BLACK EAGLES

by Leslie Lee

SAMUEL FRENCH, INC.
45 West 25th Street   NEW YORK 10010
7623 Sunset Boulevard HOLLYWOOD 90046
LONDON   TORONTO

Copyright © 1990, 1992 by Leslie Lee

ALL RIGHTS RESERVED

CAUTION: Professionals and amateurs are hereby warned that BLACK EAGLES is subject to a royalty. It is fully protected under the copyright laws of the United States of America, the British Commonwealth, including Canada, and all other countries of the Copyright Union. All rights, including professional, amateur, motion picture, recitation, lecturing, public reading, radio broadcasting, television, and the rights of translation into foreign languages are strictly reserved. In its present form the play is dedicated to the reading public only.

The amateur live stage performance rights to BLACK EAGLES are controlled exclusively by Samuel French, Inc., and royalty arrangements and licenses must be secured well in advance of presentation. PLEASE NOTE that amateur royalty fees are set upon application in accordance with your producing circumstances. When applying for a royalty quotation and license please give us the number of performances intended, dates of production, your seating capacity and admission fee. Royalties are payable one week before the opening performance of the play to Samuel French, Inc., at 45 W. 25th Street, New York, NY 10010; or at 7623 Sunset Blvd., Hollywood, CA 90046, or to Samuel French (Canada), Ltd., 80 Richmond Street East, Toronto, Ontario, Canada M5C 1P1.

Royalty of the required amount must be paid whether the play is presented for charity or gain and whether or not admission is charged.

Stock royalty quoted on application to Samuel French, Inc.

For all other rights than those stipulated above, apply to Ellen Hyman, 422 E. 81st Street, # 4C, New York, NY 10028.

Particular emphasis is laid on the question of amateur or professional readings, permission and terms for which must be secured in writing from Samuel French, Inc.

Copying from this book in whole or in part is strictly forbidden by law, and the right of performance is not transferable.

Whenever the play is produced the following notice must appear on all programs, printing and advertising for the play: "Produced by special arrangement with Samuel French, Inc."

Due authorship credit must be given on all programs, printing and advertising for the play.

ISBN 0 573 69301 3   Printed in U.S.A.

For Erma Campbell,
a dear friend

No one shall commit or authorize any act or omission by which the copyright of, or the right to copyright, this play may be impaired.

No one shall make any changes in this play for the purpose of production.

Publication of this play does not imply availability for performance. Both amateurs and professionals considering a production are *strongly* advised in their own interests to apply to Samuel French, Inc., for written permission before starting rehearsals, advertising, or booking a theatre.

No part of this book may be reproduced, stored in a retrieval system, or transmitted in any form, by any means, now known or yet to be invented, including mechanical, electronic, photocopying, recording, videotaping, or otherwise, without the prior written permission of the publisher.

Please note:

Mention is made of songs which are *not* in the public domain. Producers of this play are hereby CAUTIONED that permission to produce this play does not include rights to use these songs in production. Producers should contact the copyright owners directly for rights.

IMPORTANT BILLING AND CREDIT REQUIREMENTS

All producers of BLACK EAGLES *must* give credit to the Author of the Play in all programs distributed in connection with performances of the Play and in all instances in which the title of the Play appears for purposes of advertising, publicizing or otherwise exploiting the Play and/or a production. The name of the Author *must* also appear on a separate line, on which no other name appears, immediately following the title, and *must* appear in size of type not less than fifty percent the size of the title type.

Black Eagles was produced by the Manhattan Theatre Club in association with Crossroads Theatre Company at City Center Stage I on April 2, 1991. It was directed and conceived by Ricardo Khan and had the following cast (in order of appearance):

ELDER CLARKIE	Lawrence James
ELDER NOLAN	Robinson Frank Adu
ELDER LEON	Graham Brown
GENERAL LUCAS	Michael Barry Greer
CLARKIE	Raymond Anthony Thomas
ROSCOE	L. Peter Callender
NOLAN	Scott Whitehurst
BUDDY	Reggie Montgomery
LEON	David Rainey
OTHEL	Brian Evaret Chandler
PIA	Laura Sametz
DAVE WHITSON	Larry Green
ROY TRUMAN	Milton Elliott

Sets by: Charles McClennahan
Costumes by: Beth A. Ribblett
Lighting by: Natasha Katz
Choreography by: Hope Clarke
Sound by: Rob Gorton

Note: The Jitterbug Drill, as performed in this production, was developed by the choreographer, Hope Clarke, who added dance steps to a military drill. I welcome any theatre company to do the same.

Leslie Lee

CHARACTERS

ELDER CLARKIE, Black Eagle in his mid-60s

ELDER NOLAN, Black Eagle in his mid-50s

ELDER LEON, Black Eagle in his mid-60s

GENERAL LUCAS, White Officer in his early to mid-50s

CLARKIE, Black Eagle in his mid-20s

ROSCOE, Black Eagle in his mid-20s

NOLAN, Black Eagle in his mid-20s

BUDDY, Black Eagle in his mid-20s

LEON, Black Eagle in his mid-20s

OTHEL, Black Eagle in his mid-20s

PIA, Italian in her mid-20s

DAVE WHITSON, White Officer in his mid-20s

ROY TRUMAN, White pilot in his mid-20s

PLACE AND TIME

Washington, D.C., 1989
Reunion of the Tuskegee Airmen
Italy, 1944 during WWII

ACT I

The stage is DARK. A DRUM CADENCE is heard. LIGHTS up on ELDERS who stand DSC lost in memory. Sound of AIRPLANE flying overhead. LIGHTS up on stage. MUSIC up: "I'll Be Seeing You" sung by Billie Holiday. Time is the present; place is a reception for Colin Powell.

CLARKIE. Every year when we get together, everybody lies bigger than they did the year before. Nolan, by year after next, you will have defeated the entire German Air Force all by yourself.

NOLAN. I'm trying to tell you what happened. The truth will set you free, brother, if you let it.

CLARKIE. (*Teasingly.*) Yeah, but last year, from what I can recall, you said it was your second Jerry. Isn't that right, Leon.

LEON. Indeed you did.

NOLAN. Both of you fellas need to get yourselves a complete physical examination, because time has not been good to either one of you. Your minds are failing you, Black Eagles.

(Slide Projector advances.)

CLARKIE. Remember that? That day Eleanor Roosevelt came down and flew with Chief Anderson? Remember that?

LEON. Have mercy! White knuckle time! I have never seen so many of the top brass so close to a nervous breakdown in all my life. Swore that, that colored man was going to make Franklin Delano Roosevelt a widower.

(THEY laugh.)

NOLAN. Hell, there wasn't anybody in the United States Air Corps that Chief Anderson couldn't have taught something.

CLARKIE. What did the Pittsburgh Courier say? "First Lady flies solo with Negro Airman. Calls ride, thrill of a life time!"

NOLAN. Called for expansion of Tuskegee Project.

LEON. God bless her, or else we sure wouldn't have gotten over there.

(Slide Projector advance.)

LEON. That's the one. Last year in Kansas City, you said you were going to send me a copy of it and I'm still waiting. I told you I might want to use it for the jacket of my book. Man, I was a handsome devil, wasn't I? The rest of you guys don't look so bad either.

(NOLAN and CLARKIE guffaw.)

NOLAN. Like I was saying, we were supposed to stop short of Berlin and another flight group was supposed to relieve us, but nobody showed up, and Colonel Davis said, "Let's press on, Eagles!"

CLARKIE. We know all that Nolan, we were there.

NOLAN. We sighted that formation of ME-109's and we began climbing, just as the ME-109's started a gradual climbing turn. (*HE demonstrates again.*) I knew Col. Davis wasn't going to let those cats get away, so I got ready for a good fight. We climbed to 16,000 feet. It felt great. It was the first time a Jerry couldn't run away or out climb me ...

LEON. Kill time!

CLARKIE. Go get him, Eagle!

NOLAN. We closed in at about 500 yards, and that's when Jerry decided to quit the trail. They started to dive. And we reeled ... (*Demonstrating.*) ... and followed them. I guess it was about 800 yards, I gave a short burst, just as we broke through a cloud layer, and I saw Jerry spinning and burning. I pulled away, and I saw another one go down in flames. Calvin Wilson nailed him. I had my third, and Calvin Wilson got his fourth! And that's the honest-to-God truth. And if Wilson were alive, he'd tell you.

CLARKIE. Oh man, you know we're just pulling your leg. We know that story as well as you do.

LEON. Everybody knows everybody's stories as well as they do. The only difference is, it takes us a half hour longer each year to shoot the Jerries down.

(*THEY laugh.*)

CLARKIE. Well, we better get moving. The reception will be starting soon.

LEON. (*Still lost in the moment. Reciting.*)
"In machines of cold grey metal
That glinted in the sun
That roared and growled and whined and moaned
Fleet miracles that they were."

CLARKIE. (*As CLARKIE and NOLAN observe Leon, with some concern.*) Leon?

LEON. Clarkie, we changed some things, didn't we?

CLARKIE. Yeah Leon, we did. Come on now.

LEON. Back then, in 1944?! I never thought I'd see this day. A reception honoring the first black man to ever serve as Chairman of the Joint Chiefs of Staff of the Armed Forces of the United States of America. Colin Powell, a black man. Do you understand what I'm saying?

NOLAN. I hear you.

(MUSIC begins and the sound of MARCHING FEET.)

CLARKIE. How did we do it, huh? Huh? Somebody tell me.

NOLAN. By the grace of God.

LEON. Yeah, that and being twenty-two. We weren't afraid of living or of dying!

(CADENCE and MARCH begins.)

CLARKIE. We were immortal. We were young and strong, and we *knew* we were going to live forever!

LEON. People were talking about dying and going to hell, well let 'em go to hell, the Black Eagles were going to New York after the war and march in a ticker tape parade!

(Italy 1944, CADENCE MUSIC plays, YOUNG BLACK EAGLES march in and stand at attention. Enter GENERAL LUCAS. GENERAL LUCAS is facing the AUDIENCE to whom HE speaks directly. ELDERS position themselves near their younger selves and

watch the scene.)

OTHEL. To the right flank, march. Company halt.

(EAGLES at parade rest.)

LUCAS. Gentlemen. On some missions, we've lost at least twenty-five bombers to enemy fire! Two hundred and fifty men! And I can't have it! I won't have that! I'll play poker with an admiral before I do. *(Turning quickly to the audience.)* And do you want to know why we're losing so many bombers? Because white pilots are more interested in shooting down German fighters to satisfy their own egos than in defending the bombers. Farrabuttas! Bastards! They spot German planes, and they go huntin', leaving the bombers unprotected. No goddamn discipline. When you escort bombers, you stay put. You don't go chasing unless you are ordered to chase The bombers don't reach the target, my ass is on the line. I got two stars, I want three, and no prima donnas are going to stop me from getting them. And that is why I called you in here. *(Facing Eagles.)* I want you colored pilots to fly escort. I don't want you to let those bombers out of your sight. Now, there's only one hitch: Bombing missions are flown at high altitudes. It's extremely cold up there. And from what I've heard, you colored troops have a preference for hot weather. Well, the P-51 is a comfortable aircraft and I think it will work. I'm putting myself on the line, so don't screw up! Good luck, gentlemen.

(Sound—DRUM ROLL; EAGLES snap to attention. The LIGHTS fade out. LIGHTS up on EAGLES on a

mission. sound of AIRPLANES in flight; EAGLES sit in formation.)

CLARKIE. Blue One, this is Blue Leader. Bring it up fifty.
BUDDY. Roger, your last. . . .
CLARKIE. Spotting any bandits?
BUDDY. Negative on bandits.
NOLAN. Negative on bandits.
LEON. Negative on bandits.
ROSCOE. Negative on bandits
OTHEL. Negative on bandits
CLARKIE. Standby, turn three-five.
OTHEL. Roger.
ROSCOE. Roger.
LEON. Roger.
NOLAN. Roger.
BUDDY. Roger.
CLARKIE. Turn three-five.
OTHEL. Roger, Wilco.
ROSCOE. Roger, Wilco.
LEON. Roger, Wilco.
NOLAN. Roger, Wilco.
BUDDY. Roger, Wilco.
CLARKIE. Hold tight now, hold tight.

(There is a pause, extreme STATIC and then ANTI-AIRCRAFT FIRE and the noise of EXPLODING SHRAPNEL are heard. CLARKIE'S voice emerges through static suddenly.)

CLARKIE. Uh-oh, here comes the first flak,

gentlemen! Get ready for it.

ROSCOE. Jesus Christ, they're unloading like hell on this one, aren't they?

NOLAN. The bastards have got the exact range with it.

BUDDY. They know our approach path. Jesus, that one was close!

OTHEL. Damn those guys aren't serious, they're see-ree-us! Don't have no sense of humor down there at all!

CLARKIE. Hold tighter, Eagles. It's hell up here, but hold tighter!

LEON. Shit's so thick, you can get out there and walk on it!

OTHEL. I ain't walkin on nothin.

ROSCOE. They're shooting their load, shooting their load! It's all over the joint.

LEON. Close, close, close, close, close, fellas!

CLARKIE. Press on, Eagles, press on!

OTHEL. Press on!

CLARKIE. We're committed to the run, and we're taking the big boys all the way in. Keep the formation tight and show 'em how it's done. So press on.

OTHEL. The man said "Press on!"

ROSCOE. Let's do it, let's do it!

BUDDY. To the target!

LEON. Right to the target! Jesus Christ—mean bastards down there! Mean!

OTHEL. Flak, flak, go away, come again another day!

CLARKIE. This is Blue leader. The bombers have almost completed their run. Ten seconds to rendezvous. Standby to pick up the big boys.

ROSCOE. This is Blue Five. One accounted for and two slowpokes just completing their run.

CLARKIE. Blue Five, immediately rejoin the main group. You know the procedure: stragglers are on their own.
ROSCOE. They just need twenty seconds.
CLARKIE. Negative Blue Five, that's a negative!

(Large EXPLOSION.)

ROSCOE. Jesus Christ!

(ROSCOE is shaken violently and slumps in his seat, comatose. The sound of a PLANE, diving is heard.)

OTHEL. Blue Five! Blue Five! Come in, Blue Five!
CLARKIE. Pull up, Blue Five, pull up!
BUDDY. Roscoe, get out of there, man! Bail out!

(ROSCOE slowly regains consciousness and looks dazedly around. HE grabs the controls and comes out of the dive.)

OTHEL. He's pulling up. He's pulling up!
LEON and NOLAN. Hey, what's going on? You all right, Eagle? You okay?
ROSCOE. (*Shaken.*) I'm all right. I'm okay. Let's keep going!
CLARKIE. You heard what the man said, let's fly!
BUDDY. All the way! All the way! Here come the Eagles! Here we come!
NOLAN. Let's fly, let's fly!

(FLAK sound begins to subside.)

CLARKIE. (*Hiding his anxiety.*) Good job, Eagles. Good job. Now let's get these boys back home the way we brung 'em.

(The LIGHTS fade out, and then rise in the barracks. ROSCOE enters, tired, a bit shaken. HE sits on the cot, distant for a moment, reflective, then picks up Julius.)

JULIUS. Rough one, huh?
ROSCOE. Yeah, pretty close. Wasn't sure I was going to make it, Julius.

(HE shudders, thoughtful. JULIUS watches him, compassionately.)

ROSCOE. I was scared...

(Beat.)

JULIUS. I hate to say it —
ROSCOE. So don't.
JULIUS. —I know how you're feeling, but I could've told you so.
ROSCOE. Hey, you ought to be glad I brought you with me, you little ingrate.
JULIUS. Oh thanks, thanks a lot! Did you ask me whether I wanted to come over here? Hell no, you stuffed me into your duffel bag with the rest of your moldy gear, and that's all there was to it. How'd you like to ride three thousand miles with *your* face stuck in *my* jockey shorts? I want to go home.

ROSCOE. We can't, all right? I get a little homesick sometimes, but we have a war to fight.

JULIUS. What's this "we" stuff, Masked Man? You almost made me an endangered species, in case you don't know it. Taking me up on that stupid mission. Getting me shot at. Bullets whizzing all around me. Flak on my right, flak on my left, flak on top of me, flak underneath me. A piece of flak almost took off my nose. Another piece of flak almost took off my ear. Another almost got my arm; another, my leg. And I'd hate to tell you what the next piece almost took off. I told Lucille before I left I'd come back in one piece, and that ain't the piece I want to leave over here.

ROSCOE. Oh come on, Julius, don't you want to go home a hero?

JULIUS. Hey, boss, I keep telling *you:* I'm a lover not a fighter.

ROSCOE. Think of all the war stories you can tell Lucille when you get back.

JULIUS. I'd rather make up my own, thank you —with two feet on the ground. Let's get one thing straight, I'm not ready to be an orphan yet. So you watch yourself up there or else you're going to have Julius the Terrible to deal with.

ROSCOE. Yeah, I'll tell that to the Jerries.

(OTHEL, LEON, CLARKIE, AND NOLAN enter. THEY are tired and fatigued. ROSCOE abruptly stops talking to Julius, so the others can't hear.)

CLARKIE. Where were you at de-briefing, man?
ROSCOE. I ... skipped it. I was ... beat.

CLARKIE. You can't do that, Roscoe. The rest of us are beat too. You have to be there like everyone else ...You OK?

ROSCOE. I'm all right.

CLARKIE. You sure, Roscoe? You need to see the doctor?

ROSCOE. No. I'm OK.

OTHEL. All I can say is Praise God! Thank you, Jesus, for bringing us out of the valley of the shadow of death! That was a big assed valley today!

LEON. Hey, Roscoe, don't do that again, man, scaring us half to death.

CLARKIE. And we're not going to have it, right fellas?

NOLAN. Roscoe was getting the job did, fellow Eagles. I didn't say, getting it done, I said he was getting the job did. Now you know the job's been done.

OTHEL. Thanks to you, Eagle, we still haven't lost a bomber.

CLARKIE. Yeah, but we almost lost a couple today, and him too.

NOLAN. You're not trying to tell me that he screwed up today?

CLARKIE. We're supposed to stay in formation.

NOLAN. The man was doing what we're supposed to be doing. We're escorting the hell out of the bombers. Nobody can touch them.

CLARKIE. We're supposed to follow orders, Nollie.

NOLAN. He was following orders, dammit—bringing a couple of stragglers home. Before long, we won't be able to take a breath without somebody telling us when and how to do it.

ROSCOE. He's right, Nollie. I screwed up. I should

have stayed in formation. That's what counts.

NOLAN. What'll count for something is doing what we're trained to do—dive bombing, strafing, hunting and chasing Jerries. What will count for something is getting some kills like the white boys. That's how the top brass, the politicians and everyone back home determines who's a hero over here. Like that guy after the Great War, Eddie Rickenbacker. It's the scalps you bring back home. Now that's what counts, okay?

LEON. Do you really think they are going to let any of us pickaninnies ride down Broadway in New York City after this war, with confetti floating down, bands playing, folks screaming and hollering, and white chicks blowing us kisses! It'll be a cold-assed day in hell before they let that happen.

ROSCOE. Somebody tell me please, what the hell I'm doing over here, then.

CLARKIE. You like to fly. How about that?

ROSCOE. Hell, I can fly back home in peace and quiet.

NOLAN. You can, huh? How many airfields are you going to be able to take off and land on, huh? How many airfields did Chief Anderson get run off because he was a colored man? Hell, it's not this war we're all about, it's for the history books to record that Negroes can't fly a lick. Now that's your answer.

CLARKIE. Well I don't care what you guys say, we don't have a damn thing to be ashamed of. We're doing a hell of a job over here, and I'm saying, I'm proud of it.

NOLAN. And I'm saying, I want to fight. I came over here to battle the Jerries, just like the white boys, not to be some sitting duck, who can't pull the trigger on his own gun.

CLARKIE. We're all frustrated, Nollie. I mean, I'd like to get some kills too, but if I don't, it doesn't matter, because I'll have done exactly what they asked me. They're waiting for any excuse to send us back. Like Buddy. Where the hell is he? Now you see, that's what I'm talking about.

OTHEL. Hey, he always gets back.

LEON. He's supposed to be here right now.

CLARKIE. One of these days he's really going to screw us up. They'll throw him in the stockade, and we'll end up on a troop ship in the middle of the Atlantic Ocean on our way back home.

OTHEL. Okay, look, Eagles. It boils down to this. If we keep doing what we're doing the right way, we can prove all the doubters wrong. So let's stay on the straight and narrow path, gentlemen. All right?

(OTHEL picks up Leon's unattended diary and starts to read. LEON makes a grab for it.)

LEON. Come on, Othel, that's personal.

OTHEL. Leon, there's nothing personal over here. Right, Eagles? (*Reading.*)
 "In the bright chill of autumn afternoons,
  Young, dusky, dark-skinned boys..."
Hey, that sounds nice. Pretty.

(The others agree. LEON is embarrassed. HE grabs the diary back.)

OTHEL. I wish I could write like that. You fellas want to hear the only poem I ever wrote?

CLARKIE & OTHERS. Not really.
OTHEL. (*Overly dramatic.*)
"Roses are red, bed bugs are black and blue,
I love you, shoobie, doobie, doobie doo!"

(The OTHERS laugh.)

LEON. Man, you are out of your mind!
JULIUS. Great poetry. Good stuff! I'm really moved!
OTHEL. That's right, go ahead and laugh. But I remember the night I whispered that sweet poem into Devita Leonard's sweet ear.
NOLAN. And she threw up!

(THEY laugh.)

OTHEL. (*Ignoring them.*) We were in her basement, and the lights were down low, and I was trying to make my move on her, but she was resisting. I had run out of tricks, strategy, and options. I was at my wits end. What to do? I had spent days and weeks on my strategy to get this prized example of feminine pulchritude to succumb to my advances —

(The OTHERS laugh, hoot, and guffaw.)

OTHEL. All of a sudden, the words were there. As if by fate, as if by magic, they came, boldly emblazoned in my mind. And I threw them gently into her soft, pristine ear: "Roses are red, bedbugs are black and blue. I love you, shoobie, doobie, doobie doo!"

(The OTHERS crack up.)

OTHEL. And within seconds of those tender words being uttered—I mean, seconds—Devita Leonard was mine! Mission accomplished. Kill time! You see what happens when you stick to your program, Eagles?

NOLAN. I wonder what it's going to be like, you guys. That first kill.

OTHEL. I hear some guys have erections and come in their pants.

JULIUS. Now that's what I want. Bring on that first kill, and then the second, and then the third.

ROSCOE. Shut up, Julius, you're embarrassing me, man.

NOLAN. I'd write home and tell my dad. They won't be able to stand him at the Bethel Baptist Church, he'll be bragging so much. And he's the preacher.

OTHEL. They'd probably have a parade in my hometown. Right down the main street. Waving their flags, singing patriotic songs, majorettes showing their pretty little legs.

ROSCOE. My dad would break out the cognac. He loves the stuff. He brought back a couple of bottles from the Great War. He'll, open one up, pour a little bit in everybody's snifter, and then cork that boy back up, and wait for me to come back. And then we'll do the whole damn bottle in. And he'd be so proud.

CLARKIE. We're not doing too bad for a bunch of darkies who're supposed to be an experiment.

OTHEL. We'll get our chance. Someone will get the first one. And then when it rains, it'll pour. We've got to stick together, because it's about more than us, you know that Eagles. It's about your family, Nollie, and yours too, Roscoe, and mine and everybody in here. It's about helping to change things back home. You know? Hey, we're helping to pave the way, Eagles. You hear what I'm saying?

CLARKIE. Loud and clear!

OTHEL. Well all right! (*New approach.*) You know, I heard that there are some colored boys on this base who think they can do the Jitterbug Drill better than we can.

ROSCOE. Say what?

CLARKIE. Who is putting out that bold faced lie?

LEON. A sho-nuff lie, because every Eagle on this base in his right mind knows who's the boss, right fellas?

NOLAN. Who is it? Come on, spit it out!

OTHEL. I heard some guys from 99th Ground Crew are going to try and challenge us.

JULIUS. No way, Eagle, no way!

OTHEL. Going to try and topple us from our throne. Us, the meanest and baddest bunch of flyers, escorters and jitterbuggers this side of heaven or hell.

CLARKIE. We are handsomer than they are. We even smell better.

JULIUS. The crème de la crème of United States Air Corps!

LEON. Tell the truth, Julius.

OTHEL. There's no way they can beat us, can they?

NOLAN. No way, no indeed!

OTHEL. Let me hear it. I said, "Who's the boss?"

ALL. The 99th!

OTHEL. Who's the king?

ALL. The 99th!

OTHEL. And who can't be beat?

ALL. The 99th!

OTHEL. Then, let's get it going! The drill! Yeah, the drill.

(THEY begin to dance, a combination tap dance drill, neatly and expertly choreographed. It is exuberant and happy. BLACKOUT.

The LIGHTS rise on a small bedroom. A stack of old records and an equally old phonograph sit in the center of the room. There is also an unfinished clay sculpture. It is late at night. PIA lies asleep in a rickety looking bed.

BUDDY stands at the window, staring out, as MUSIC, being played by a mandolin, VOICES and LAUGHTER can be heard distantly. PIA rouses suddenly and looks drowsily at BUDDY, who turns and watches her fondly.)

BUDDY. Ciao.

PIA. Ciao, bello. Buddy, why do you sit at the window? Why are you not asleep?

BUDDY. I don't know. My mind wouldn't turn off, so I got up. *(Beat.)* The music, it's pretty.

PIA. Sometimes, the signore, at the piazza, they stay up late and drink vino, and tell stories about "the old days." It's nice, but "the old days" keep everyone awake.

BUDDY. It's the same everywhere, isn't it? Where I come from, the old men sit around on the street corners, playing checkers, drinking cheap vino. The same thing, Chicago.

PIA. Si, si, Chicago. Bang, bang! Chicago, I have many relatives who go to Chicago.

BUDDY. I really like it here. I do.

(*Song "Bello Ciao."*)

PIA. *Cittadino Italiano.* I think I'm going to declare you Italian citizen.

BUDDY. I'm beginning to feel very Italian. You don't belong here.

PIA. Be angry then, and curse the bombs that fell from the sky and killed my family.

BUDDY. Yes, I am angry about that, dammit! Nobody deserves to be alone.

PIA. But I manage, Bud-dee. I am alive, Grazie a Dio.

BUDDY. Yeah, thank God for that. Or else I would never have seen you on that bus. I couldn't keep my eyes off you. You looked beautiful. You looked scrumptious! When you got off at San Savero, I knew I had to get off too. I mean, what choice did I have after you so obviously flirted with me?

PIA. Oh Buddy, that is not true. I would never do nothing like that.

BUDDY. (*Continuing to tease.*) I wonder how many other soldiers have gotten off that same bus with you?

PIA. (*Pulls away from him.*) Do not accuse me of that please. It is not true.

BUDDY. Hey, signorina, I'm teasing. I'm just teasing.

PIA. There was only one American before I met you.

BUDDY. Yes, your white soldier. The one who told you that we colored soldiers have tails and climb trees. Nice guy. Hey, when I leave here, he doesn't come sneaking through the back door, does he?

PIA. (*Pulls away angrily.*) If I am a bad woman, then you should also be ashamed of yourself for being with me.

BUDDY. Hey, come on. I'm sorry Pia. I'm jealous.

(HE goes to her and tries to hold her. SHE pulls away.)

PIA. What right do you have to speak to me like this?
BUDDY. I said, I'm sorry.
PIA. He has not been back here for several months now. He is gone. I am certain I am only a memory to him, just like I will be to you.
BUDDY. Hey, come on, don't talk like that. I have a big mouth, and I just put my foot into it.

(HE grabs her, kissing her. SHE pulls away, goes to the phonograph, puts on a BESSIE SMITH record. It begins to play. SHE stands and listens, her back to him. HE watches her, genuinely sorry.)

BUDDY. It's just that ... well, you're better than that guy. He didn't deserve you. But I'd never leave you. Just disappear, as though you never existed at all.

(HE tries once more to embrace her. SHE turns her back to him. Frustrated, HE begins to dress and pack, as SHE sits and begins to sculpt.)

BUDDY. (*Listening.*) Bessie Smith. What are you sculpting?
PIA. *Non lo so.* My hands have yet to tell me. My father used to say this to me. He was a *scultore*, and he teaches me to do the same thing. He teaches me to love to do this, and to love Bessie Smith. He knows everything about Bessie Smith. He says she is a *miracolo da dio*. A

miracle from god. She and Caruso, they are the best, they are angels. There is no one in America like Bessie Smith, is there?

BUDDY. Of course not.

PIA. *Ecco.*

(THEY exchange smiles. HE pulls up a chair and joins her at the table.)

BUDDY. You really miss your father, don't you?

PIA. Si, my father was a good man.

BUDDY. I'm sorry, I really am.

PIA. Grazie. (*SHE looks at his sculpture.*) Oh that is a beautiful goat!

BUDDY. A goat! It's my dog at home—Chico. Thanks a million.

PIA. Oh, *mi dispiace.* Perhaps Chico must be a goat. He makes a beautiful goat.

(THEY are silent a moment.)

BUDDY. It just seems impossible, you know? That wars are fought on nights like this one. You, me, Bessie Smith, old men outside drinking vino and singing. You can see the stars. I mean ... that's the only thing ... the only thing that makes me afraid sometimes to go up there and dodge all that flak. Hey, I'm a wild guy up there in the air, Pia. You should see me. I can do a lot of things with that ship of mine that a lot of pilots, Black Eagles or white guys, can't do. But sometimes ... sometimes that flak is sailing up at me, and I get afraid of dying, Pia. Of dying ... on nights like this one, nobody in this world should die. Nights like this are nights when the whole world should be alive ...

(The LIGHTS fade. An EXPLOSION is heard suddenly.)

    NOLAN. There it is. Here it comes.
    OTHEL. It's a decoy, Nolan.
    NOLAN. I've got it in my sights.
    CLARKIE. Nolan, you're breaking formation.
    ROSCOE. Nolan get back here.
    NOLAN. I'm going for it. I'm going for it.
    OTHEL. Nollie, get back in formation.
    NOLAN. It's in my sights.
    LEON. Nolan!
    NOLAN. Got him.
    ELDER NOLAN. Damn!

(LUCAS enters suddenly.)

    CLARKIE. Ten-hut!

(THEY snap to attention.)

    LUCAS. Fighter pilots are fighter pilots regardless of race, color, creed or personality. Your primary job is to protect the bombers. Do you understand that? If it is reported to me that any one of you has left the bombers to chase enemy aircraft, I will not only ground that pilot, but I will strongly recommend that the 99th be subject to a court-martial and sent back home. Is that clear?

(CLARKIE and the OTHERS sit morosely and distantly,

the tension cutting.)

LUCAS. As if you didn't have enough problems already. (*HE grabs a report from his desk.*) I have a report here from Colonel William Momyer, the commanding officer of the 33rd Fighter Group. He says—(*Reading.*) "The 99th air discipline has *not* been completely satisfactory. Their ability to fight as a team has *not* yet been acquired. Their flying formation has been satisfactory until jumped by enemy planes, and then the squadron seems to disintegrate." (*HE scans the reports further, pacing, visibly upset.*)
ELDER LEON. It was an out-and-out lie. The 99th did not disintegrate.
NOLAN. You had to see him go down, Roscoe. You were right on my freaking wing!
ROSCOE. I didn't see anything. I repeat: I didn't see anything.

(YOUNG NOLAN watches the OTHERS in renewed disbelief.)

YOUNG NOLAN. And the rest of you guys are going to sit there and tell me you didn't see him go down either, right?
CLARKIE. We were protecting the big guys like we were supposed to.

(NOLAN shakes his head, disbelievingly.)

YOUNG NOLAN. Sonsofbitches!
ELDER NOLAN. I'm not saying we didn't make some

mistakes.

ELDER LEON. Of course we did, but all the training in the world can't prevent mistakes in your first aerial mission. Oh no!

ELDER NOLAN. The truth of the matter is, they wanted us to fail.

LUCAS. "The 99th is not of the caliber to display aggressiveness and desire for combat that are necessary for a first class fighting organization." Jesus H. Christ, what the hell did I need all this for? (*HE goes to the window and stares thoughtfully out.*)

ELDER LEON. Now how the hell could we "display aggressiveness and desire for combat," when our express orders were not to go after the German fighters were, huh? Somebody tell me.

(*LUCAS turns to face Elder Leon.*)

ELDER LEON. Our command, sir, is to escort the bombers and that's exactly what we've trying to do. Back home, people are automatically assuming we aren't producing, because we're colored. And you're well aware of that, sir.

ELDER NOLAN. We're damned if we do, and damned if we don't.

ELDER LEON. No sir, it's remarkable that these men have kept their morale at all. It's really remarkable.

ELDER LEON. No sir! It's not fair, and it's not right!

LUCAS. I want to remind you that there are plans being discussed by General Arnold to disband the 99th as a fighter unit and send it back to the states for routine convoy cover. Be aware, gentlemen. Be very aware.

(LUCAS exits.)

NOLAN. I'm asking you guys if you saw the Jerry go down. He was on fire plain as day, heading for the ground. I hit the bastard! I got a kill, and none of you guys wants to verify my kill. I think that's pretty shitty, if you ask me.

LEON. We didn't see him, Nollie.

NOLAN. You sonsofbitches. You freaking bastards are just jealous, that's all. You're jealous because I'm the first one.

ROSCOE. Nobody's jealous of anybody, man. But I'll tell you what we are teed off about—

NOLAN. Tell me you saw the Jerry go down dammit! Tell me, goddammit!

OTHEL. You were chasing Jerries, Nollie. You know damn well what you did.

ROSCOE. *(To Nolan.)* You left a hole in our formation, Eagle. You left a big gaping hole in our formation because you couldn't keep your freaking cool.

NOLAN. I'm telling you, he was coming at me.

LEON. He was shit, Nollie, he wasn't even close. You went after him.

NOLAN. I did what I was trained to do. I shot him down! I shot the sonofabitch down.

CLARKIE. Shut up, Nollie, just shut the fuck up!

NOLAN. Fuck you! I'm going over to the officer's club and celebrate what I shot down with the white boys. They know what the hell I'm talking about.

OTHEL. We're not allowed over there, Nollie.

LEON. It's off limits. You know that.

CLARKIE. Get the hell back here, Nollie.

LEON. We can't afford any trouble. There's too much at stake. Maybe one of us should go over and stop him.

ROSCOE. He almost fucked up our record today, the idiot. We still haven't lost one goddamn bomber. I'm pretty proud of that record. If I had any sense at all, I'd have shot his black behind down myself.

LEON. You think he's going to do it?

ROSCOE. Do what?

LEON. Go over to the Officers' Club.

ROSCOE. Christ, I don't know. We all ought to be going over there. The white boys have a club. He probably won't go.

LEON. How do you know he won't?

ROSCOE. I don't know that he won't. I just don't think he will. He's a hot head, but he knows. He's just blowing off steam. Don't worry about it.

ELDER NOLAN. I didn't really think I was doing wrong. I really didn't.

ELDER CLARKIE. I know.

ELDER NOLAN. I was doing what I thought I had to do.

ELDER CLARKIE. I know.

(LEON goes to bed. The LIGHTS in the barracks dim. BUDDY appears and prepares for bed. His rustling awakens CLARKIE, who seeing him, rises quickly from his bed and grabs him and pulls him to the door, and shoves him outside.)

CLARKIE. Shhhhh!
BUDDY. Hey, what the hell are you doing?
CLARKIE. Shhh! You'll find out. We have to talk.

(THEY are outside, CLARKIE releases him.)

CLARKIE. You don't give a hoot whether you get here on time or not, do you? You just do what you damn well please, don't you?

BUDDY. I don't know what the hell you're talking about, Clarkie. I always come back. What's your problem, man?

CLARKIE. Your attitude, that's my problem. Okay? We have a freaking job to do over here, man.

BUDDY. Oh now wait a minute, wait just a minute, partner. You're not going to tell me I don't do my job, are you?

CLARKIE. You do your job, but it's for good old Buddy. If we screw up, we screw up for every colored person back home, and the whole country, too.—We've got a lot of pride in my family, man. And that's the way I was brought up. If we say we're going to do something, we ain't going to do it half-assed. We do the best goddamn job we can.

BUDDY. I understand that. If I didn't, I wouldn't be here.

CLARKIE. You have to care more, Buddy. You have to care more about us and the race, man—

BUDDY. You can stop preaching, all right?

CLARKIE. No, man. Not until you get some sense in your thick skull. Do you hear what I'm saying, Buddy?

BUDDY. How can I not help but hear you?

CLARKIE. You see? The way you answer? It's your attitude.

BUDDY. Do you want me to grin when I say it? Okay, I'm grinning. A nice big grin. Cheese!

CLARKIE. I'll beat the shit out of you, Buddy. I swear

to God I will.

BUDDY. Look, I'm beat, I want to sleep. I'll get back here on time

CLARKIE. Mean it, Buddy.

BUDDY. Cross my heart and hope to die.

CLARKIE. Buddy, mean it, dammit!

BUDDY. (*Making a sign.*) Jesus Christ! Scout Sign of Honor then. Will you accept that? It's good in any language. I mean it, Clarkie. I won't screw the Eagles up. I won't. Cross my heart and hope to die, Scout sign of honor, and a grin. What else do you want?

CLARKIE. Nothing, that's enough isn't it?

(THEY return to barracks. BUDDY finishes preparing for bed, CLARKIE picks up Julius.)

BUDDY. (*Eyeing Julius.*) Hey! What the hell are you doing with Julius.

CLARKIE. Practicing. Roscoe's teaching me. (*As Julius.*) I got three letters from my sweetheart today, and I feel marvtastic!

BUDDY. You're really terrible, you know that?

CLARKIE. (*As Julius.*) I was getting worried. I thought some other knucklehead was trying to move in on my turf.

BUDDY. I mean, you are really ... bad!

CLARKIE. (*As Julius.*) As soon as I get back home, the little lady and I are going to get married.

BUDDY. Are you serious?

CLARKIE. Of course I am. Lisa and I have been going together since we were in grade school. It was given by everybody that we'd get married. I knew since the first time I met her, in sixth grade.

BUDDY. Come on, Clarkie, nobody knows it then.
CLARKIE. I'm telling you, I did,
BUDDY. And you never dated other girls?
CLARKIE. Not really.
BUDDY. What's "not really" mean?
CLARKIE. No, I haven't. Just Lisa, okay?
BUDDY. You mean to tell me—
CLARKIE. Not really.
BUDDY. I didn't finish.
CLARKIE. Not really.
BUDDY. You mean you never made love to any other girl?
CLARKIE. Not really.
BUDDY. Stop saying that, will you? How the hell can you "not really" make love to another girl? Either you do or you don't.
CLARKIE. Maybe one other girl.
BUDDY What the hell do you mean maybe? That's as bad as "not really."
CLARKIE. Joanne Caldwell, but only once, and I felt as guilty as hell, and I didn't enjoy it.
BUDDY. And you don't feel like you've missed out on anything?
CLARKIE. Not really.
BUDDY. You're saying it again.
CLARKIE. Not really.
BUDDY. You said it again. Well, Christ, if you knew you were going to get married all along, why didn't you just get married when you were in the sixth grade ? You'd have saved a lot of time and money.

(ROSCOE awakens and comes over.)

ROSCOE. What the hell are you doing with Julius? (*Grabbing him away.*)

CLARKIE. Practicing.

ROSCOE. Only when I say so, dammit. You just don't take him without asking me.

CLARKIE. You were asleep, and when I saw Buddy, and Julius started telling him about me getting married.

ROSCOE. But Julius can't tell him that, he doesn't even know it.

CLARKIE. I told him.

ROSCOE. You can't be Julius, only I can be Julius. You have to be somebody else.

CLARKIE. Then why did you let me practice with him then?

ROSCOE. Just to practice, not to be Julius.

CLARKIE. But that's Julius, dammit. I can't be anything else than what the stupid dummy is.

BUDDY. I really don't believe all this.

ROSCOE. How about believing that you are going to mess us up around here, all right?

CLARKIE. I told him.

BUDDY. He told me.

ROSCOE. People have their eyes on us—

CLARKIE. I told him.

BUDDY. He told me.

ROSCOE. I mean, Jesus Christ, Buddy don't you know what this is all about?

CLARKIE. I told him. And it doesn't make any sense, only you can be Julius. Julius is Julius, whether it's you me, or anybody else.

ROSCOE. He's me! Be somebody else!

CLARKIE. And the Italian woman is going to send you and the rest of us down the toilet, man.
BUDDY. Oh sure, of course, if we lose the war, it's going to be an Italian woman's fault. Well, goodnight, fellas, nice chatting with you.

(NOLAN stands at the entrance to the barracks.)

ROSCOE. Just wise up. There's a greater good than lounging in bed with Italian women.
CLARKIE. I told him.
LEON. He told him.
ROSCOE. Well, I'm telling him again.
BUDDY. Well, I'll tell you I have really been told. And will you please tell everybody else I've been told so I don't have to go through being told again?
CLARKIE. (*Follows him; to Roscoe.*) You can keep your stupid dummy, man.

(NOLAN enters.)

ROSCOE. You're damn right I will. Julius—Hey dummy, you do that again, and you're firewood.

(ROSCOE turns. OTHEL and NOLAN enter around each other's shoulders.
THEY laugh, and then quiet as THEY enter the barracks. ROSCOE and NOLAN exchange a glance.)

ROSCOE. Othel, is he all right?
OTHEL. Yeah ... He's fine ...
ROSCOE. Hey thanks, Eagle.

(THEY exchange a thumbs up sign.)

OTHEL. *(As an afterthought.)* He just wanted to fly, that's all. He just wanted to fly—

(ROSCOE does not respond.
Blackout. PLANE sounds.
The LIGHTS rise fully on ROSCOE, who sits in the barracks with CLARKIE, NOLAN, and LEON. THEY are morose and fatigued, still dressed in their flying uniforms.)

ROSCOE. He told me that he had developed engine trouble. That's when I saw the smoke. I told him to head back to the base. He said, "No, I'm going to finish the run, we started together, we're going to finish together." But the next thing I knew, his plane is diving. That's when I lost sight of him.
LEON. I saw his ship going down.
NOLAN. Parachute?
LEON. I didn't see it.
NOLAN. Me neither.
ROSCOE. You guys sure?
LEON. Maybe he got out. I don't know.
NOLAN. He might have. He could have.
CLARKIE. He probably did.
ROSCOE. Jesus Christ, what the hell's going on? Eddie Lathan spins into the runway, blows up just taking off. A simple routine mission.
LEON. It was just an accident, man. It almost happened to all of us. Those are machines out there we fly, no matter

how much we personalize them, and give them names and stroke them and kiss them, and all the things we do. They're just machines.

ROSCOE. And now Othel.

CLARKIE. That was Othel's fault. He should have returned to the base. Stupid. There are enough Jerries up there trying to blow us out of the air, and he does something like that. Wait till I see that big headed rascal.

ROSCOE. He's probably in Trento right now, singing and dancing ...

NOLAN. ... showing them the Jitterbug drill. He can fly, you all! You listening to me, huh? Do you hear me? The man can fly! The closest thing to a real eagle this side of hell, man. The man can fly!

CLARKIE. We know that. But he didn't know his limits. It was bound to happen. That's the problem with you guys. The white man puts you in something that flies, and you don't know how to act.

NOLAN. Hey, what's with this "you" stuff.

CLARKIE. Yeah, "you." I'm safe and I've always been safe.

NOLAN. Yeah, so we noticed. You might even call it not having any guts.

CLARKIE. Hey, Eagle, I know you're not talking about me.

NOLAN. If the helmet fits, wear it, man.

CLARKIE. I hope you aren't saying I'm a coward.

NOLAN. You heard what I said.

CLARKIE. (*Standing, threatening.*) I'm asking you something, Eagle. I'm asking if you're trying to tell these people I'm a coward or something?

NOLAN. I said what I had to say.

LEON. Come on you guys, settle down.

CLARKIE. Hey, we can go up in the air right now, you no flying monkey—right now, and I will personally show you which one of us doesn't have any guts.

NOLAN. That's exactly the reason Colonel Davis had you relieved and made Elmore Rogers Operations Officer—because you couldn't handle it.

(CLARKIE stands and moves toward Nolan, but ROSCOE steps in front of him.)

CLARKIE. You are full of shit, eagle!

ROSCOE. What are you guys, officers in the United States Air Corps, or a bunch of recruits?

CLARKIE. It's bullshit, and he knows it. They brought Rogers in because he had more experience than I did. It didn't have a damn thing to do with whether I could fly or not.

LEON. The man's right, Nolan.

CLARKIE. The only person I'm worried about is Colonel Davis. He's commanding the Eagles, and he told me, I was a good flyer, and I wouldn't be a Black Eagle if I couldn't fly well. You washed out at Tuskegee, if you couldn't fly. And you know it. And being safe doesn't have anything to do with being chicken. I'll bet you one thing, colored man, I will get my first Jerry a long time before you do.

NOLAN. Keep on dreaming.

CLARKIE. And you know it. You know it. You never could shoot straight. I was the top aerial gunner at the Eastern Flying Command, and the third best gunner at the that Air Corps meet at Elgin Field. I beat the white boys, and I beat the rest of you in here. I beat all of you. And I'll get my Jerry first over here too.

NOLAN. So get your stupid Jerry first, all right? Be my guest. Get it tonight, get it tomorrow, get all you damn well please. It doesn't change what I said. Othel may have taken a chance, but at least he took it.

CLARKIE. He just went down, Nollie. You get it? The man just went down. (*Pushes Nolan.*)

NOLAN. But he has guts. Do you get that?

(*HE pushes Clarkie back. The TWO MEN go for each other and begin to fight.*)

NOLAN. Nobody can say Othel isn't the boldest colored man in an airplane they ever saw. But I'll be damned if I'll ever say that about you!

(*BUDDY, LEON, and ROSCOE break in to stop and separate them.*)

CLARKIE. And I'll be damned if I'll ever be able to say that about you either, so that makes us even. (*To Leon and Roscoe who are restraining him.*) Get off me! Get your hands off me! Let go of me Goddamnit!!

(*HE wrenches away, then moves to a corner and stands. BUDDY enters. The FIVE MEN stand, frozen for a moment.*)

BUDDY. He's dead, you guys. Othel.

(*The OTHERS look at him stunned.*)

BUDDY. A couple of guys saw his ship hit the water, about five miles from the shore. No parachute, no nothing, just a lot of fire and wreckage. He's passed on, Eagles.

(ROSCOE breaks out of the group and goes to Julius. The LIGHTS dim as ROSCOE moves into his own SPOTLIGHT, picks up Julius, then sits.)

ROSCOE. Julius, are you asleep? I need to talk. Remember Aunt Clara? I was really crazy about her. I liked her better than any of my relatives. She was the only one I didn't hide from when they came to visit. She used to pick me up when I was a little kid, and whirl me in the air above her—around and around and around. I felt like I was flying, and I didn't want her to stop. "Don't stop, don't stop, Aunt Clara! Fly me all the way to the sun please!" And she'd laugh, way down deep, and she'd say, "Oh, no child, this old plane is coming in for a landing right now! You'll be able to take your own self up there one day." And when I got my license, I took her up. She didn't want to go at first. I had to beg her. Finally, she went. And as we took off down the runway and into the air, she started to laugh, like a young girl. "Take me up higher and higher and higher, son. Fly me all the way to Heaven!" She didn't want to come down, "Because it was so peaceful, so free, so close to God." She died not too long after that. I never had a chance to take her up again. But sometimes, even now, when I'm up there, I can hear her laughter, resounding all over the sky. And I know that whenever I take off, she's up there waiting for me ... *(HE places his head against Julius' and closes his eyes as as the LIGHTS fade out.)*

End of Act I

ACT II

(The LIGHTS rise on YOUNG EAGLES who are in barracks, relaxing.
THE ELDERS enter. MUSIC can be heard behind them.)

LEON. We were approaching the target at Anzio, and as usual, the German Gunners were blasting away—beautiful red and orange bursts of fire and smoke. Death, but still beautiful, sending huge hunks of flak, floating lazily up into the air, as if in slow motion, so slow it seemed that if you just reached out, it would slide gently into your hand. But it was a delusion. A volley of it slammed into my ship and tore my landing gear off. I heard another bang and when I looked back, my tail was coming apart. That lazy, floating, harmless flak kept slamming into me. I dropped down in my seat behind the armored plates to protect myself. But just then, flak sliced through the door, like a knife through soft butter, and smacked into my leg. Jesus Christ, it hurt—hurt like I've never been hurt before. I called Nolan and I told him, "I'm hit, my ship's hit!" And he said, "Hold on, partner, hold on!" I kept dropping. I managed to clear the top of a mountain by only a couple of feet. And then, all of a sudden, I hear Nolan and Clarkie over the intercom, singing. *(Singing.)* "Swing low, sweet chariot, coming for to carry you home!" And two guys—you two, wild, crazy, beautiful, daring, adventurous fools, got on both sides of my ship, placed their wing tips under mine, lifted me, and flew me home! And that's what being a Black Eagle is all about.

CLARKIE. I'll never forget the time I got hit by an ack-ack burst. I went into a dive at four thousand feet. I tried to pull it out, but I couldn't control my elevators. The ship was lost. I tried to climb out of the left side of the cockpit, but the slip stream knocked me back into the plane. Then, I tried the right side, and I got halfway out, when the slip stream caught me and threw me away from the ship where I dangled until the wind turned the ship at about one thousand feet from the ground, shaking me loose. I must have reached for my ripcord six times before I found the damn thing. My chute opened right away, and I landed in a cow pasture

NOLAN. (*Overlapping Clarkie.*) I saw Clarkie's ship get hit and start diving. I knew he couldn't control it, and I started yelling, "Come on, Clarkie, man, get out of there! Get out!" And finally I saw his chute open. He was a couple thousand feet from the ground when it opened.

CLARKIE. A couple thousand? What do you mean a couple thousand? I must've been nine hundred feet from the ground, and that's a big difference.

NOLAN. I was there too, Clarkie. I saw you. You were at two thousand feet.

CLARKIE. Man, if I were at two thousand feet, my *damned* heart wouldn't have been pounding like a sledgehammer. Nine hundred feet!

LEON. You two, Lord have mercy!

NOLAN. All right, you want nine hundred feet, then nine hundred feet, for pete's sake.

CLARKIE. It isn't what I want, but whether it's the

truth or not.

NOLAN. *Anyway*, I shouldn't have, I know it, but I followed him down, and I don't know what possessed me—some instinct, some compulsion, but I knew I couldn't leave him there in that cow pasture. I brought my ship down, landed hard, and he saw me. Sniper fire started to rain all around us. "Come on, man, get the hell in here!" He scrambled into the cockpit and then I raced along that lumpy ground back into the air, with bullets whining and whizzing all around us. And it wasn't about being a hero, it was about saving a fellow Eagle. Now how are you going to forget that, huh?

(THEY begin to leave.
As THEY exit through the barracks,
ELDER LEON reaches out to touch Younger Leon.)

ELDER CLARKIE. Leave that boy alone!
ELDER LEON. What are you talking about, I am that boy. He just doesn't have my arthritis yet.

(ELDERS laugh and exit.
(LIGHTS up on YOUNG NOLAN, LEON, ROSCOE, CLARKIE and BUDDY who are reading, writing letters, and listening to music.)

LEON. Lena Horne, I mean, there she was! On stage, in front of us! I mean—real! I mean, pretty, and real, and gorgeous, and scrumptious and foxy! Lena Horne, you all! You hear me! I am sorry, fella I have to get out of the war and go home to where Lena is! That's all there is to it! Don't I, baby? *(HE moves to the pinup poster and kisses it.)*

CLARKIE. Hey, man, get your mangy lips off my woman!

BUDDY. Your woman? Man, you're supposed to be getting married.

CLARKIE. I am. But Lena Horne is the only woman alive that can make me change my mind!

NOLAN. There she was, right in front of us on that stage. Only ten feet in front of us, singing her sweet little song. Oh, sing to me, Lena, baby, sing to me!

(HE begins to sing. The OTHERS join in.)

JULIUS. She sure lit a fire under my caboose. I'll tell you that.

NOLAN. I'm weak. I don't think I'll ever be able to fly again, Red Tails. I don't have the strength. And it's terminal!

LEON. There is a God, gentlemen. That woman proves, there is a God!

(Enter WHITSON and TRUMAN.)

CLARKIE. Ten-hut.

NOLAN. You gents sure you have the right place?

CLARKIE. Yeah, the "Officers" club is in the other direction.

WHITSON. (*Still hesitantly.*) This is the ... colored officers' barracks right?

ROSCOE. Yeah?

WHITSON. We've got the right place then.

(BUDDY and the OTHERS stare at them curiously.)

BUDDY. For what?
WHITSON. For what?
BUDDY. Yeah, right place for what?
TRUMAN. The colored officers' barracks. We just thought we'd stop by.
BUDDY. I'm saying, for what?
TRUMAN. Just dropping by.
BUDDY. Oh, I see ... dropping by. A social call, right?
WHITSON. Right, a social call.
BUDDY. For what?
WHITSON. I'm Dave Whitson, 82nd, and this is Roy Truman, also 82nd.
TRUMAN. Glad to meet you fellas.

(THEY stand awkwardly, looking at each other, self-continuously exchanging introductions.)

WHITSON. Mind if we sit down?
LEON. No, go ahead. Help yourself.

*(WHITSON and then TRUMAN sit.
LEON and the OTHERS stand awkwardly.)*

TRUMAN. Hey, have a sit down.

(LEON and the OTHERS look at each other, and then CLARKIE begins to laugh. The OTHERS join him. TRUMAN and WHITSON look at them curiously, then begin to laugh without really knowing why. LEON and the OTHERS sit finally.

BUDDY goes to the phonograph and takes the needle from the record.)

TRUMAN. Hey, you don't have to do that. Those are some hot licks.
WHITSON. Yeah, sounds real jazzy.

NOLAN. (*Looks quickly at the others, trying to restrain a smirk.*) You know, we've been trying to think of a word for it all afternoon, haven't we, fellas?
ROSCOE. Indeed we have.
NOLAN. And you guys walk in here and with in seconds you've got it, "jazzy" that's it, isn't it guys.
CLARKIE. Yea, jazzy's certainly the word, thanks fellas.
WHITSON. You're welcome. We just got here from North Africa to join the 79th Fighter Wing on this base. Not long ago. We've heard a lot about you guys, so Roy and I decided we'd come over and meet the Black Eagles.
CLARKIE. Yeah, so what were you guys doing over there in North Africa?
TRUMAN. A little mopping up.
LEON. You get any kills?
WHITSON. Yeah, I got three. Roy got a couple.
NOLAN. What was it like, the kill ... your first one?
WHITSON. Oh. man. there must have been fifty Jerries up there that day, and they—
TRUMAN. Five, he means five. Take off the zero, Five.
WHITSON. Yeah, five. That's what I meant to say. But it seemed like fifty. Right?
TRUMAN. You could say that.

WHITSON. And they're coming from all directions. Six o'clock, four o'clock, one o'clock. Every damn where—

TRUMAN. Like hornets, just like a bunch of nasty hornets, out to get you.

WHITSON. And so, I got into it with this one ME-109.

NOLAN. No, I mean, what was it like? What did you feel like?

TRUMAN. Unbelievable. I mean, un-fucking believable!

WHITSON. It's hard to describe. A feeling I never had before in my whole damn life. Exhilarated. I don't know—ecstatic! I wanted to scream, I was so fucking, unbelievably happy!

TRUMAN. I did. I screamed my goddamn fool head off! (*HE screams.*)

WHITSON. I don't know, it was when I scored my first varsity touchdown in high school. You guys know—that first T.D.!

NOLAN. (*And the OTHERS.*) Yeah, yeah—the first one. Touchdown! Six points! Crossing the goal line! Crossing the goal line!

TRUMAN. Yeah, when I tossed in two points at the buzzer. and we won the State Championship. I went crazy. I mean, I just went nuts, I was so excited! Right? Am I telling it true, huh? You guys've been there right?

BUDDY. Yeah, right ... exactly. You guys want a beer?

(*Beat.*)

WHITSON. Yeah, sure.

TRUMAN. I'll second that.

ROSCOE. No, no. You know what I feel in the mood for? I feel in the mood for some cognac.

NOLAN. I was just going to suggest the same thing.

ROSCOE. We bring it out on special occasions, for special guests. Right, fellas?

LEON. That's the way I was brought up.

NOLAN. Isn't that something? I was brought up the same way.

CLARKIE. Me, too. Come one, let's break out the grog. You guys don't mind, do you?

WHITSON. No not at all. Sounds great.

TRUMAN. I'll second that.

ROSCOE. (*Moves to a small cabinet and pulls out a bottle of cognac.*) Now this is the real deal, gentlemen. This is genuine cognac. You gents ever taste any of it

TRUMAN. Haven't had time to. We've been in North Africa, mopping up there.

WHITSON. Everything you drink there tastes like camel piss.

BUDDY. (*Jokingly.*) I've never tried it.

ROSCOE. Well, there's no camel piss in this bottle. No indeed. Hey, somebody get the snifters.

BUDDY. The snifters?

ROSCOE. Yes, Lieutenant, the snifters. The cognac snifters, the ones we always use for distinguished guests.

CLARKIE. Yeah, Buddy, you know ... the distinguished guests snifters.

BUDDY. Oh yeah, the snifters! Oh yeah, how could I be so stupid? The snifters!

TRUMAN. Hey, you fellas don't have to get fancy for us.

WHITSON. Hell no, we're just as regular as everybody else.

ROSCOE. No, no, no, we insist. Buddy, break out the snifters.

BUDDY. (*Bowing.*) Your wish is my every command, sire. (*HE goes to the cabinet and pulls out paper cups and holds them aloft. In a phony French accent.*) Voila, zee cognac Snif-tairs!

(*The OTHERS laugh, along with WHITSON and TRUMAN.*)

NOLAN. Sorry, gents, that's about all we can afford in this club. I'm sure they have real sho' 'nuff real snifter at the other place, don't they?

WHITSON. Hey, paper cups are fine. I drink out of 'em all the time.

TRUMAN. Yeah, me too. I don't go for all that Fancy Dan stuff.

(*ROSCOE begins pouring, and BUDDY distributing.*)

CLARKIE. Yeah, a guy can get too civilized in this world. We can't have that.

LEON. (*To Truman.*) Hey Truman, You're not related to Harry, are you?

TRUMAN. The Vice President?

LEON. That one ...

TRUMAN. Everybody asks me that. No, not that I know of.

LEON. Yeah, because if you were, I'd have to be nice to you.

(EVERYONE laughs. WHITSON stands.)

WHITSON. You fellas mind if I propose a little toast.
ROSCOE. Go ahead, take a stab at it.
WHITSON. *(Hesitating, thinking.)* To the Black Eagles, and to the 82nd, may they fly together, united against their common enemy, the Third Reich, and bring glory and honor to our country, the United States of America.
TRUMAN. Hear, hear, I'll drink to that.
CLARKIE. *(With less enthusiasm.)* Cheers.

(ROSCOE and the OTHERS follow suit.)

TRUMAN. Hey, this is good stuff, You fellas are right about that. Christ, here we were in North Africa, drinking camel piss, and you guys are over here living in the lap of luxury with cognac. The War Board's going to hear about this. *(Laughing.)*
NOLAN. *(Facetiously.)* Well, we've got to get something out of this war. Right, Eagles?
ROSCOE. I'll drink to that.

(CLARKIE and the OTHERS murmur agreement.)

WHITSON. I've wanted to meet you guys for a long time.
ROSCOE. What are they saying about us, huh? In your circles?
CLARKIE. Yeah, what's the word on us?
TRUMAN. Hey, you're good flyers.

WHITSON. Real good flyers. Some guys are surprised as hell, and some of 'em still don't want to admit it, but I think it's bullshit. Because, we all ought to be flying together all the time. Now that's what I think.

NOLAN. What are you guys, rejects?

TRUMAN. I agree one hundred percent. There are guys in this Air Corps who wouldn't want to fly with you fellas, but we're not among them, right, Dave.

WHITSON. That's right.

NOLAN. Yeah, well, we ought to be flying together, but we ain't.

WHITSON. Maybe one day we will ... It's got to happen. If you fellas keep up the job you're doing, flying escort, then it has to happen.

BUDDY. Hip hip hooray for flying escort!

LEON. Love that flying escort!

CLARKIE. Yes, indeed, that's exactly why I wanted to fly. Escort!

TRUMAN. Hey, the big guys have to get through. And you fellas are the reason they're doing it. It's pretty damn amazing when you think of it. Not one bomber lost. You guys haven't dropped one bomber, that's what's so amazing.

NOLAN. Why, because we're a bunch of jigaboos? Is that what folks are saying?

CLARKIE. Nolan—

TRUMAN. Hey, come on, I didn't mean it that way. No, no, I mean, if you fellas were white guys, it's still be amazing. That's what I'm talking about. I wasn't trying to infer anything else.

WHITSON. Hell, no.

BUDDY. You have to pardon the Lieutenant. It doesn't

take much of this cognac to get him started. Happens every time.

TRUMAN. Yeah, no offense, Lieutenant. I mean, amazing is amazing, no matter who it is.

WHITSON. That's right.

NOLAN. You know, we can fly. I mean, we can really fly! You understand what I'm saying?

WHITSON. Hey, I'll put my money on it.

NOLAN. No, you're not listening to me. I mean, fly! Really fly!

WHITSON. Yeah, that's what I said.

BUDDY. No, no he means Fly! You see the way it rolls off my lip, Fly! We can do more than just fly escort for the big boys up there. We are flyers, just like you guys.

TRUMAN. Hey, so who's arguing?

CLARKIE. You see, you guys fly the ground missions. And you do a good job. And nobody's saying you don't.

LEON. No, you do all right.

CLARKIE. But you're the ones who get the Jerries. You make the kills, because we can't break formation and go after them. You guys go back to the States the big heroes—

WHITSON. Oh come on, guy, everybody's a hero in this thing.

TRUMAN. Everybody's got their part to do. Right? Huh?

NOLAN. Hey, why did you guys come into this Air Corps, huh? Why? I'll tell you: so you can throw bullets into the Jerries and blast them out of the sky. You want that freaking kill, that's why you came in. And you can't tell me any different.

WHITSON. You guys aren't getting any?

NOLAN. What the hell do you think we're saying to you.

BUDDY. Ease up, Nollie it's not their fault.

NOLAN. Who the hell said it was?

LEON. No kills, nothing. Nothing, nothing, nothing, that's what he's saying.

TRUMAN. Yeah, okay, I get it. But that must mean you're doing your job.

ROSCOE. It also means we aren't getting any kills, and we're in this Air Corps for the same reasons you white fellas are.

WHITSON. But you have to remember something. We've probably got a little more experience than you have.

ROSCOE. How long have you been in?

WHITSON. Almost a year.

ROSCOE. Well, we've been in two years, all of us.

NOLAN. That's right, two years.

LEON. Two long years.

CLARKIE. And how long did you guys go through flight training?

(WHITSON and ROY look at each other.)

WHITSON. Six months.

ROY. Yeah, six months.

CLARKIE. Us? A whole year!

ROSCOE. A whole year! They got you guys out in six months, and kept us in a whole year because we're an experiment.

LEON. And we were ready a hell of a long time before.

NOLAN. You're damn right we were. But they didn't know what the hell to do with us. We logged more hours in flight training than a lot of you guys have done in the air over here.

ROSCOE. Did either of you guys do any flying before you joined up?

WHITSON. (*Looking at Truman.*) No ...

ROSCOE. What about you, Harry?

TRUMAN. Roy, it's Roy.

ROSCOE. I'm joking. What about you? Any flying before you came in?

TRUMAN. No not really ... no ...

ROSCOE. So where's the experience, huh? Hey, I was a licensed pilot before the war, and there were some other Eagles who were, too.

WHITSON. I meant, in general. In general. I'm talking about, you know, white guys on the whole—flying. The Wright Brothers, you know. We've been up there a lot longer than you have.

CLARKIE. Hey, I'm not going to fight you about the Wright Brothers, but you two guys have been up there less than we have.

TRUMAN. (*Feeling the cognac.*) Yeah, but we can fly too.

CLARKIE. Of course you can. You're supposed to know how to fly. If you didn't, I wouldn't feel the least bit sorry for you.

TRUMAN. Like birds, we fly like birds.

BUDDY. Hey, wait a minute, you're talking to eagles—Black Eagles.

TRUMAN. Well, you're talking to White Eagles!

ROSCOE. Terrific! That's good. So we're all eagles, and we both can fly, but we should all be doing the same damn thing. It should be equal, but it's not equal. It's not equal in that freaking lousy club over there, and it's not equal in the air. There's a white air corps and a colored air corps and that's the long and the short of it.

TRUMAN. (*Grabs the bottle of cognac and holds it out to Roscoe.*) Here, have some.

ROSCOE. I'm full up.

TRUMAN. No, the bottle, take a swig from it.

ROSCOE. No!—Hell, no you don't do that to good cognac. You nurse it, you savor it.

LEON. Hey, come on, when the hell did you become an expert on cognac? You couldn't even spell it before you came over here.

ROSCOE. Hey, White Eagle, don't let him fool you. Some of us do know how to spell.

LEON. (*Whispering.*) But not cognac.

(OTHERS laugh.)

ROSCOE. My father knows a lot about cognac. I told you that. He taught me. You hold your glass, like this. Pretend this is a snifter. And, you hold it like this. (*HE demonstrates with a paper cup.*)

BUDDY. (*Effeminately.*) Oh my, fellas, you hold your snifter like this. (*Exaggerating.*)

(The OTHERS laugh.)

ROSCOE. It doesn't have anything to do with being a homo, you idiot. It's about having a little class, which, I might add, you are sorely lacking. Cognac is special. It's like a classy woman. Now that's your problem, you don't know how to handle a classy lady.

BUDDY. I assure you, I know the difference between a stupid paper cup and a woman, Roscoe.

TRUMAN. Come on, take a swig, just a little one.

ROSCOE. No way, White Eagle, It would be sacrilegious.

CLARKIE. (*Grabs the bottle.*) Hell, I've always been a little short on religion. Lemme have it.

(TRUMAN hands him the bottle, HE starts to drink, but ROSCOE stops him.)

ROSCOE. Come on, You'll ruin it.

CLARKIE. (*Wrestles it away.*) Roscoe, somebody needs to take your temperature. This is a bottle of cognac, not some damn woman! (*HE takes a swig.*) My, my, my! OoooWeee! Love that cognac!

TRUMAN. (*Grabs the bottle from Clarkie and takes a swig.*) There, you see? Did you see it?

LEON. See what? What the hell were we supposed to see?

TRUMAN. What I just did.

LEON. Yeah, I saw what you did. So what?

TRUMAN. I just took a drink from the same bottle as this Black Eagle and I didn't wipe the bottle off like a lot of white people would do.

NOLAN. (*Applauding, facetiously.*) All right, all right, stop the presses! Read all about it! White Eagle drinks from same bottle as black—history in the making!

TRUMAN. No, no—a lot of white guys wouldn't. (*HE takes the bottle and drinks from it again, then shoves it toward Leon.*)

TRUMAN. Come on, drink up.

ROSCOE. You guys aren't serious, are you? You can't be. There's plenty of other stuff you can do that to, but not to cognac.

TRUMAN. Come on, drink up, Eagle.

LEON. (*Grabs the bottle.*) The man's a guest in my house. If he tells me to drink, I drink. That's the way I was brought up. It wouldn't be polite. I was raised better. (*HE takes a big gulp.*) O! Mamma mia! Arrivederci, Roma! (*HE hands the bottle to Whitson.*) Your turn White Eagle.

(*WHITSON instinctively makes a move to wipe the bottle off. TRUMAN stops him.*)

TRUMAN. You can't do that, Whit, those are the rules!

WHITSON. It was a natural impulse, that's all. A natural impulse.

CLARKIE. I don't know now. I don't know. I think we might have ourselves a little "nigger in the woodpile" here.

WHITSON. Hey, come on, don't use that word. I hate that word.

CLARKIE. No more than I do.

WHITSON. It was just a natural impulse. I learned it at home. My parents, you never drink from the same bottle. It's health, that's all. From anybody. My own mommy even.

TRUMAN. Are you going to drink or not, White Eagle?

WHITSON. I'll drink the shit. I'll drink it. I'll get germs, and I'll die, but I'll drink it. (*HE drinks it, then hands the bottle to Nolan.*) All right, you satisfied? WoWee!

NOLAN. I'm only doing this because I'm a little

thirsty, that's all.

(HE takes a swig, then hands it to Buddy, but TRUMAN grabs it and takes a quick swig, then hands it to Buddy.)

TRUMAN. We can't break the chain. Have to keep the chain.
BUDDY. Jesus Christ, I'm half blind already.
TRUMAN. Then you have another half blind to go. Go to it, Black Eagle.

(BUDDY takes a long swig. TRUMAN again takes the bottle and hands it to WHITSON, who is "flying" now, along with the OTHERS.)

WHITSON. Black Eagles, living in the lap of luxury, and we're drinking camel juice.

(HE drinks, TRUMAN grabs the bottle and shoves it at Roscoe.)

ROSCOE. Hell, no, forget it!
TRUMAN. Come on, Black Eagle, drink up!
ROSCOE. Drop dead, White Eagle, you don't guzzle down cognac that way. It's really disgusting. It really is.
CLARKIE. Christ, don't we sound like a bunch of Indians? White Eagle, Black Eagle ...
NOLAN. Come on, Roscoe, show the man you aren't a bigot. Show him. Go ahead.
ROSCOE. I don't have to swill this stuff down like an imbecile just because you idiots don't have any better sense. It's like a beautiful woman ...

(The OTHERS begin to yell at Roscoe to drink.)

NOLAN. *(Chanting.)* Black Eagle, Black Eagle ...

(OTHERS join.)

ALL. Black Eagle, Black Eagle...
ROSCOE. *(Giving in.)* Oh for Christ's sake.

(HE grabs the bottle, drinks, as the OTHERS cheer.)

TRUMAN. All right! White and Black Eagles together! That's what we are!
NOLAN. You see, you White Eagles are the ones. You're the ones. You need to tell that General—General Lucas and the rest of the top brass about this bottle of cognac, if it's important to you. *(Beat.)* Is it important to you, White Eagle?
TRUMAN. You're damn right it's important. Of course it's important.
WHITSON. My sister brought home this little colored girl once, and my folks had conniptions! I mean, they had conniptions! But I fully supported my sister in her actions, and expressed that opinion to my parents, who promptly grounded both of us.
NOLAN. *(Pauses a beat, then turns to Truman.)* You see, you White Eagles have got to pitch a bitch. You White Eagles have got to kick and scream and cause all kinds of ruckus, until your fellow Eagles get some kills, so we can finally prove to these people that we are the real deal! Do you understand? Some Kills! Are you going to do it, White

Eagles? Lemme hear you!

TRUMAN. Gonna do it, Black Eagle! Gonna do it!

WHITSON. Yeah, go up into the man's face and tell him, "General, you have to straighten up and fly right and let my fellow Eagles get themselves some kills!"

CLARKIE. That's right, your cut-rate, boon coon, buddy, buddy Eagles!

TRUMAN. Cut-rate, boon coon, buddy, buddy Eagles!

BUDDY. White Eagle is going to shout it all over God's Heaven, aren't you? Aren't you? Let my people go and get themselves some kills!

WHITSON. Shout it all over God's Heaven!

LEON. (*Begins to sing raucously.*) "I got a robe, you got a robe, all God's chillen got a robe!"

(*OTHERS join in singing.*)

LEON. "When I get to Heaven, gonna sit on my throne and gonna shout all over God's Heaven, heaven, gonna shout all over God's Heaven!"

ROSCOE. (*As LIGHTS dim, cradles empty cognac bottle.*) You do not get drunk on cognac you stupid people. You nurse it, you savor it! Maybe you get a little high. You get a little buzz. You get a warm glow, you get mellow. But you do not get drunk. (*Beat.*) I can't believe it, I can't believe this shit!

(*HE watches the others then grimacing, feeling out of it, HE joins them in the drunken circle. After a moment, THEY begin to chant softly.*)

BUDDY. (*And the OTHERS.*) Black Eagles, Black

Eagles, Black Eagles!...

(Chant grows intense and powerful, becomes a round.
A LIGHT goes up on GENERAL LUCAS, who stands watching them.
THEY come to stand at attention, face the audience and begin slowly marching in place as LUCAS begins his monologue.)

LUCAS. Damn it, damn it! I've received an order, gentlemen, from upstairs. It seems I've got to pull you off escort duty. You're going into the battle for Anzio. They need every fighter pilot they can their hands on. If I had my way, I'd keep your right where you are. I'll probably have a mutiny on my hands. All the pilots, bombardiers and navigators who take those buckets of bolts up there fall on their knees every goddamn night thanking the Good Lord you're up there with them. They'll probably name their kids after you. Think of all the white kids running around with names like, Hannibal, Alfonso, Luther ... Spurgeon. Yeah, there's one—Spurgeon.

(HE begins to move among them, as THEY don flight uniforms, intense DRUM CADENCE accompanies these actions.)

LUCAS. Our objective is to isolate the battle area to prevent enemy forces from bringing up reinforcements and supplies than could be a successful counter attack. You men will support the ground troops by bombing supply depots, bridges, harbors and roads—and strafing enemy trains and concentrated troop deployment. You will engage

Nazi fighters more frequently and in greater numbers than you've done flying escort. There will be swarms of them, there, trying to defend those positions and installations. I want you to pay close attention and remember something. The German fighter pilot is among the best in the world. That's something you won't know until you've flown against him. They are good flyers, no matter how much you hate the arrogant bastards. And some of you boys are going to get shot down, so stop romanticizing this stuff.

Joe Louis might have knocked out Max Schmeling, but your Joe Louis never had to go up against a Focke-Wulf, a Messerschmidt, or a Stuka. If he had, you'd still be crying in your beer. There'll be great sorrow in your ranks, because each time a pilot goes down, it hurts, no matter what the comic books might say. *(Beat.)* So gentlemen, you are going to get your little wish. You wanted the Nazi's, well you've got 'em.

(LIGHTS change, intense, pounding MUSIC begins along with the sounds of PLANES and MACHINE GUN FIRE; LUCAS, WHITSON and TRUMAN exit;
EAGLES assume flight formation; ALL are in silhouette a spot will come up on EACH as HE tells his story.)

NOLAN. I pulled up behind the Messerschmidt, you see? And I gave him two quick bursts from my gun. I hit him and it made a sharp dive for the ground. I followed him. But as I approached the ground, I met a heavy barrage of fire. They hit my ship, but I'm sorry, I was hunting trouble, and I smelled blood. I threw some more fire power into him. And suddenly, he burst into flame—into a brilliant, orange and red, engulfing flame—the most beautiful sight I had ever seen in my whole life. I had my kill. Praise God. I had my first, freaking kill!! Othel, this one's for you. Oh, man, that's what this freaking war's about!

OTHERS. BLACK EAGLE!

(LIGHTS out on NOLAN and up on LEON, who addresses the audience.)

LEON. These Jerries rolled up under me, you see? Like this. *(Demonstrating.)* Well, I rolled over, slammed everything forward, dove and zeroed in on an FW-190 at about 450 miles per hour. And then, I gave him a short burst of fire, but I was leading him too much. So I waited. Sometimes you have to wait. You can't be too eager. You have to take your time, cat and mouse, cat and mouse, cat and mouse—and then, he peeled out of a turn. I gave him two, long, two-second bursts. *(HE demonstrates with SOUNDS.)* And his engine burst into flame. And then, he exploded! Blam! Just like that. One big, giant, sudden explosion, and he went straight for the ground. But I got my kill, dammit! I got my kill. Shit, man, I got me a kill!

OTHERS. BLACK EAGLE!

(LIGHTS out on LEON, and then up on CLARKIE, who addresses the audience.)

CLARKIE. I pull out of my dive, and I start climbing. That's when I notice this Stuka heading down at me, blasting away. I break away from him into a cloud, but as I come out into the clear, the bastard is there waiting for me. He makes a pass, but he misses. Now I'm in control. I'm on his tail, and he begins snaking from side to side. (*Demonstrating.*) But every time the sonofabitch turns, I give him a short burst of fire. And, on the fourth one, his left wing begins to smoke. Oh baby! And then I see the rudder come flying off—in two pieces. He bails out. His chute flies open, but his ship goes straight down and smashes into the Anzio Beach. Oh baby! Wooooooeeee! Baby, Baby, baby! I got him! I got him! You hear me? I got my first kill! Oh shit, it's about time! Oh baby!

OTHERS. (*Facing him.*) BLACK EAGLE!

(LIGHTS out on CLARKIE up on ROSCOE.)

ROSCOE. These German planes came at me. Closing in on me from all directions. It was what they called the German "Wolf Pack." Just like a pack of wolves. They gang up on you. And these guys were determined to make the kill. I made a dive.

(OTHERS face front.)

ROSCOE. (*Demonstrating.*) And I looked back. One of them was still on my tail. I was headed toward Berlin, and I knew I didn't want to go that way. I tried to shake him. I quickly cut my speed. And the sonofabitch overshot me— And now I'm on his tail. He was in range. I opened fire. I gave him two long bursts, and then a couple of short ones, and he started tumbling—(*Demonstrating.*)—tumbling, tumbling to the ground. And then he smacked into it, spewing fire and smoke. Oh man, I was happy. My heart was racing and pounding like a drill hammer! I could fly! I knew then I could fly! Oh shit, man, I could fly! And that

Jerry before he smacked into the ground knew it too. My first kill. I got my kill! (*Laughing.*) Break out the cognac, Dad! And keep it out!

(The LIGHTS go out on ROSCOE and then up on BUDDY.)

OTHERS. BLACK EAGLE!
BUDDY. I opened fire on him at long distance. But I missed him. But an ME109 turned in front of me. I got him in my sights, and I started firing away. His tail exploded. I let him have a couple of more bursts, and he nose-dived (*Demonstrating.*)—and headed straight down into the ground. I wanted to scream, I was so happy, but I didn't have time. Another ME 109 turned in front of me. (*Demonstrating.*) I rolled on him, and I fired. He began to smoke and then he fell, in a dive, toward the ground and plowed right into it! Two of them! I'll be damned! Two of 'em, just like that I screamed my fool head off. I took a little time off from the war, and I screamed my fool head off, and then I started to sing:

> "Off we go into the wild blue yon-der, Climbing high into the sun...

(OTHERS join in.)

> Here they come zooming to meet our thun-der Atom boy, give 'em the gun...
> Down we dive spouting our flame from un-der
> Off with one hell of a roar

We live in fame
Or go down in flame
Shout! Nothing can stop the Army Air Corps"

(CLARKIE, LEON, NOLAN, and ROSCOE all join BUDDY upstage and embrace.
CHEERING and LAUGHING THEY exit as the LIGHTS dim to black.
The LIGHTS rise on PIA who is sculpting.)

BUDDY. *(Entering her flat.)* Pia! Pia! I got my kill! Pia, do you hear me?
PIA. You shoot a Jerry down, huh?
BUDDY Girl, I shot two of them down!
PIA. Si, bravo!

(HE rises quickly and goes to the phonograph and puts on a record. MUSIC erupts.)

PIA. Buddy, what are you doing?
BUDDY. You'll see, you see. The guys'll have a fit if they find out it's gone, but as long as I bring it back, they'll get over it.
PIA. Who is it?
BUDDY. You don't know who that is? That's Jimmy Lunceford.
PIA. Jim-mee, *come sil dice*?
BUDDY. Jimmy Lunceford. He's colored, and it's one of the best bands in the world. Right up there with Glenn Miller and Tommy Dorsey, and Benny Goodman, and Charlie Barnet, and those guys. You hear it? That's what they call a Big Band Sound. Ten, twelve maybe even

fifteen musicians. (*HE begins to dance to the music.*) Hey, signorina, come here, let me show you how we dance in America. I'll show you how to Jitterbug.

PIA. You are talking about bugs?

BUDDY. (*Going to her, pulling her to her feet.*) I'll explain later. Come on, let me show you.

PIA. Jitterbug?

BUDDY. All right now, let's go. Do what I do now. Come on, watch me now!

PIA. (*Laughing.*) Oh, this jitterbug is a very strange dance!

BUDDY. You'll learn it, you'll learn it!

(*HE begins whirling her about. SHE squeals in laughter and in some fear.*)

PIA. Oh, Bud-dee, you must not let me fall!

(*HE whirls and twirls her in the most extreme of movements. SHE laughs happily.*)

PIA. How do I dance the Jitterbug? Am I good?

BUDDY. Here we go again. Watch out now, here we go! (*HE swings her again and throws her over his back.*)

PIA. *O, santo cielo! Mamma mia!*

(*The MUSIC ends. Gasping for breath, SHE collapses on the bed, breathless. HE dances over to the phonograph and removes the record.*)

BUDDY. So, how do you like the jitterbug, signorina?

PIA. Oh, it is *pericoloso*! Dangerous. That is what they

dance in America?
PIA. That's right.
PIA. One must practice *gimnastica. Acrobata*!
BUDDY. No, one must just love to dance.

(HE stops dancing and stands watching her. SHE looks at him and then away, almost shyly.)

PIA. Why do you look at me like that?
BUDDY. Because I want to ... Just because I want to. Is that all right?
PIA. Si, if you want to ...
BUDDY. God, it's so beautiful here. It's *bello, bello, Molto bello*!
PIA. *Molto bello*!
BUDDY. *Molto bello*! Everything's so emotionally expressive, so permanent. I like that. Grazie. A thousand thank yous, signorina.
PIA. *Perche*? For what?
BUDDY. For making me aware of it.
PIA. Certainly you would have noticed without me.
BUDDY. But I wouldn't have appreciated it. I mean, it was never part of what I was in America. I was walking from the bus station, and I began to see things that I never seen before—Antiquity!... the motifs, facades, their elegance and exuberance. It overwhelmed me. I stood there tears streaming down my face as if, as if I had seen a *miracolo da dio*. I'm really thinking about staying here, Pia.

(SHE turns away.)

BUDDY. What's the matter?

PIA. Bud-dee, you are like a *cavolino*. A young colt. *Allegro, vivace!* [Frisky] You are filled with *engergia*.

BUDDY. Yes, yes, that's right. (*HE rises, grabbing her and whirls her about.*) And what's wrong with that? I have found the pasture, and I like it out here!

PIA. But there are many pastures, Bud-dee, and there are many things in the pasture. It is all new, and you must give yourself time to *esplorare*. I am new, the pasture is new the grass is new, and the sky is new. It is nice but it is a ... *fantasia* ... a fantasy—a dream—

BUDDY. (*Grabbing her and sitting her down.*) Now listen to me, just listen to me. (*Beat.*) Where I come from, in America, there are lot of things a colored person can't do. People don't treat us the way you do here. We're not equal over there. We're still at the bottom of the ladder.

PIA. Listen, I will not be the experiment with you as you are with the Americans. I do not want that. If you are *sul serio*, if I am not just your new toy, if I am someone who is permanent in your life, then that is good. Buddy, I love you, but you must love me, not because I am new, but because I am me. Do you understand me, Buddy?

BUDDY. One day a long time ago I realized that the whole damned world belonged to me. Not just the streets of Chicago. And no one would let me have it. But now, I've got it. I am going to stay here, and I'm going to drink vino, and sing Italian songs, and dance with you for the rest of my life, signorina! I love you, Pia.

(*HE rises quickly, pulling her to her feet. HE begins to sing an Italian song and dance with her. As THEY dance, SHE looks away from him sadly, uncertain of his certainty.*

The LIGHTS rise on ROSCOE, NOLAN, LEON WHITSON, and TRUMAN, who stand expectantly around, as CLARKIE holds a canister.)

NOLAN. Come on, Clarkie, what the hell is it?
ROSCOE. (*As Julius.*) Yeah, why are we standing around here waiting for you to open up a canister?
WHITSON. You know, that's a good question!
ROY. (*Jokingly.*) Come on, Clarkie, the tension is killing me!
LEON. (*Also joking.*) Frankly, it's putting me to sleep.
CLARKIE. Now that I have your undivided attention, we can begin. I want you to know I've been saving this little baby here for a long time despite numerous temptations to dispose of it. But my sense of—
NOLAN. Man will you kindly get on with it!
CLARKIE. My sense of history allowed me to resist the strong urge that would have ruined this very moment.

(JULIUS pretends to be snoring very loudly.)

LEON. I've got some strong urges, but I'd hate to tell you what they are.
CLARKIE. In honor of our first kills, I want to share with my brother Eagles, the white ones here and the colored ones. (*HE begins to open up the can.*)
WHITSON. Finally!
CLARKIE. (*Opens up the can and pulls out a small bottle of Coke.*) Voila! Coca Cola!

(The OTHERS are genuinely taken aback.)

NOLAN. What the hell?
ROY. I'll be damned! Do you see that, Whit?
ROSCOE. Where the hell did you get that?

(BUDDY enters.)

CLARKIE. I found it when we were in Casablanca. I don't know, one day, there it was among the rubble—
NOLAN. Come on!
CLARKIE. Hey I'm serious. It was there, and I started to open it, but something told me to wait for history!
JULIUS. He couldn't find a bottle opener that's why he didn't drink it!
BUDDY. History my ass!

(OTHERS laugh.)

CLARKIE. All right, here it is, chilled and ready! And here we go ! Here we go. (*Taking a bottle opener from his pocket.*)
WHITSON. (*And the OTHERS.*) All right!
CLARKIE. *Voila!*

(The OTHERS applaud. CLARKIE holds the bottle up in a toast.)

CLARKIE. To the Black Eagles!
NOLAN. Our ... first kills.
CLARKIE. (*Teasingly.*) You sure about that, Nollie?
NOLAN. Yeah, yeah, I'm sure. Our first kills. And there will be many, many more!

BUDDY. Hear, Hear!

ROY. I'll drink to that!

CLARKIE. (*Takes the first sip.*) Oh, my, my, my, my, my! (*HE passes it to NOLAN.*)

NOLAN. Bless you, brother Clarkie—bless you, sire! (*HE passes it to Buddy.*)

BUDDY. Jesus Christ, that's good! I mean that is good!

(*HE passes it to ROSCOE, HE drinks, passes it to LEON. HE passes the bottle to ROY.*)

ROY. You know, I think I've just died and gone to heaven!

(*HE hands bottle back to LEON, HE then passes it to DAVE.*
DAVE jokingly makes a move to wipe the bottle off. He drinks.)

ROSCOE. Hey, what about Julius? We have to share it with Julius don't we?

CLARKIE. You put that bottle to that little dummy's lips, and both of you will be dead dummies!

(*The OTHERS laugh.*)

CLARKIE. And this is for the Eagles that didn't make it. (*HE pours a bit on the floor and downs the rest.*) We did it y'all!

(*A cheer goes up from the OTHERS.*)

LEON. We're going for broke now!

ROSCOE. That's right! (*To Whitson and Roy.*) Step aside, cool, breezes, and let the big winds blow!

WHITSON. Hey, Hey we can get a couple of bets going.

ROY. That's right, that's right!

CLARKIE. That's what I like to hear.

BUDDY. You are on!

ROSCOE. Hey, you know this is nice, all this camaraderie and stuff, but we have proved ourselves in the air. We proved it.

WHITSON. You're damn right you did.

ROSCOE. We didn't lose a single bomber when we were flying escort. Then today, we shot down thirteen Jerries! Every single one of us in here is as much a man as the other. Am I right?

TRUMAN. Goddamn right!

ROSCOE. Well, I got news, White Eagles, we can't just be brothers inside this goddamn barracks. We still aren't allowed into your lily white, Officers' Club. And here we are men together. All of us have shot own a Jerry, gotten our first kill——all of us are flyers. Aren't we now?

WHITSON. (*And the OTHERS.*) Damn right!

ROSCOE. I mean, we are some mean sonofabitchin' flyers. Well, I think it's time my Black Eagles and I went over and socialized and were "men" at the Officers' Club. I mean, those guys next door are going home for Thanksgiving turkey, cranberry sauce, and Mom's good old American mince meat pie because of *us*! And I want some thanks. I want somebody to thank me. Pat me on my back, shake my hand, and say, "Let's have a drink together." I think we should go over to that club and get that whole base to toast the Eagles. To toast our fallen brother Othel for dying so they can open Christmas presents from Santa Claus!

NOLAN. I'm with you.

BUDDY. I like the way this man talks.

LEON. Roscoe, come on, cool it.

ROSCOE. No, I think it's time. It is time, goddamn it! There are no boys in here. We're all men, and my fellow White Eagles agree!

TRUMAN. We're all men, that's right!

ROSCOE. Then, I think, since we've more than enough times offered you the hospitality of our humble abode, that you should invite us over to guest, right now, at the Officers' Club. Your humble abode. In fact, I dare you. Right now. I got my kills, I want the rest of what I've deserved since I've been over here, to drink where the hell I please. I dare you. Let's see what you're made of. Come on.

(WHITSON and ROY look at each other.)

WHITSON. Hey, it's never been us.

ROY. No, hell, no.

ROSCOE. We know that. I'm a man, dammit, just like you are. We just established that fact.

WHITSON. We agree, dammit!

ROSCOE. Well then, let's go goddammit!

TRUMAN. All right, let's go! I'm not afraid to go over there with you guys! Let's go!

ROSCOE. Let's go! Shit, let's go!

BUDDY. Let's do it!

(EVERYONE except LEON and CLARKIE begin to exit.)

CLARKIE. Hey, guys. Come on, we got our kills, and let's keep our cool now! Come on Roscoe!

LEON. Jesus Christ, come on, you guys, it's just more freaking trouble!

(The OTHERS stand and look demandingly at Clarkie. HE hesitates, then joins them.
NOLAN embraces him. CLARKIE looks at Leon.)

NOLAN. Clarkie, it's time, brother.

CLARKIE. Come on Leon, we have to go. We've got to, man.

LEON. *(Hesitates, unwillingly.)* Shit ...

(HE rises finally, joining them.
THEY start out and then suddenly freeze, coming to attention as GENERAL LUCAS enters carrying a clipboard, WHITSON and ROY move upstage right and remain at attention throughout exchange.)

LUCAS. The 99th has done well, remarkably well, and that will go a long way, but there are rules and you men must obey them. There are no "ifs," "ands" or "buts" about it. I'm not telling you to sign this regulation, the War Department is. We cannot have this kind of distraction during this conflict. I want you men to sign this statement understanding and accepting that you will be segregated from all facilities used by white officers on this base. *(HE stares hard at them for a moment, then moves toward them, holding out the pen and clipboard.)* Who will be the first to sign?

(HE holds the clipboard out to ROSCOE who hesitates.)

ROSCOE. In all good conscience, I can not sign that statement, sir.
LUCAS. *(Taken aback.)* You said what?
ROSCOE. In all good conscience, I cannot sign that statement, sir.
LUCAS. *(Staring hard at him for a moment.)* I see ... *(HE moves to Nolan.)*
NOLAN. *(Quickly.)* In all good conscience, I cannot sign it, sir.

(NOLAN and ROSCOE exchange glances.)

LUCAS. Do you men understand the full consequence of your actions? Do you? You went through hell to get here. Everyone's proud of you—your families, your people, your country. Now, you're going to throw all of that away?
LEON. *(Moves toward him and takes the clipboard, HE is about to sign then changes his mind.)* In all good conscience, I cannot sign this statement, sir

(LUCAS moves quicker now, going to Clarkie.)

CLARKIE. I can't sign it, sir

(LUCAS looks at Buddy.)

BUDDY. Neither can I, sir.

LUCAS. You can't, huh? Well, if you men want to find a place in this Air Corps, you'd better learn to follow orders, whether you like them or not.

BUDDY. Sir, this is a travesty of our rights.

ROSCOE. Sir, to sign that statement, as you request, means that we are purposely abridging our rights as officers of the United States Armed Forces.

LUCAS. I have my job to do, and I will not tolerate dissension and anarchy in my ranks.

BUDDY. (*Interrupting.*) But sir, we're officers ...

LUCAS. The Officers' Club here on this base will remain segregated according to the policy of the Air Corps and the United States Government.

ROY. (*Interrupting.*) Sir, some of us white officers wish to speak for ourselves. We have no problems sharing social and recreational facilities with colored officers.

WHITSON. I fully support that, sir.

LUCAS. (*To Black Eagles, ignoring Roy and Whitson.*) This is for your protection, and for smooth operational procedures during this conflict. I am not going to fight two wars. The one against Hitler and Mussolini is enough. Now, I order you to sign this statement. My career is on the line just as well as yours. I too, am following orders that I don't particularly like or agree with, but I am a soldier and I obey the orders of my superiors. Now, either you will sign this statement or I will be forced to remove you from this conflict and keep you under arrest until you come to your senses. The choice is yours.

ROSCOE. (*Sadly but resolutely.*) Sir, the men and I, in all good conscience, cannot sign that statement.

LUCAS. Does this man speak for all of you?

OTHERS. Yes, sir!

(The LIGHTS change. LUCAS, WHITSON and TRUMAN move off stage.
The OTHERS are now in the stockade.)

LEON. Unbelievable! Unbelievable! Two hours ago we did something most white pilots have never done.

CLARKIE. We shot down thirteen Jerries! Thirteen of the bastards, and here we sit in a freaking stockade, like we were just a bunch of common, petty thieves.

LEON. What the hell is going on? Somebody tell me, what the hell is going on?

ELDER NOLAN. It's America, come straight across the Atlantic. How's that, huh? It didn't matter what the hell we did.

ELDER LEON. I mean, marching us between lines of guards—heavily armed guards. Just like we were Nazis.

ELDER CLARKIE. That's the kind of treatment, you can expect from the Germans or the Japanese, but here it was, from your own country—the country we're fighting and dying for.

(ROSCOE begins a slow, sparse version of the Jitterbug Drill; one by one, throughout the remainder of the scene, the OTHERS join in.)

NOLAN. Maybe we're fighting on the wrong damn side.

LEON. I don't want to hear that kind of talk.

NOLAN. Well maybe we are.

LEON. We're not. We're on the right side, they just don't know it yet! That's the last thing we need to hear from anybody. Jesus Christ, fighting on the same side as Adolph Hitler? Come on Nollie, let's not let being in here scramble our brains. No, we are on the right side, but the right side has got itself a hell of a lot of problems.

NOLAN. A hell of a lot of problems.

ROSCOE. I'll stay here until I get what they owe me, no matter how much I don't want to be in here. Ain't that right Julius? You with me? (*As Julius.*) I'm with you partner.

CLARKIE. (*Almost to himself.*) I'm not sorry you know? I'm not sorry.

NOLAN. About what?

CLARKIE. Being a Black Eagle.

NOLAN. (*And the OTHERS.*) Oh no, hell no!

CLARKIE. The best thing that ever happened to me.

(The LIGHTS dim on the OTHERS and remain on LEON, who speaks softly at first, and then builds, as He recites a poem He has written.)

LEON.
We sat, often,
As young, dusky, dark-skinned boys,
In the bright chill of autumn afternoons,
Hidden among the forbidden stalks of an old man's cornfield,
Necks craned, our eyes skyward,
Spying on white men,
Who flew like eagles,
In machines of cold, gray metal,
That glinted in the sun,
That roared and growled, and whined and moaned,

Fleet miracles that they were.
Young, dusky, dark-skinned boys
Among stalks taller than we,
Agape and pining,
wishing it were we who flew,
Pretending, Flapping our arms, as if they were wings,
Which, alas, it took us no further,
Than the tips of our toes,
While the exasperated shrieks from mothers,
Who had momentarily lost their dusky, young sons,
Reverberated,
Impinging upon our fantasy,
And remotest possibility,
That, if only we could be eagles,
And stretch wide our wings,
And leap into the air,
And soar and glide and sail,
And climb so very high,
So very far,
Until we are but tiny specks in the heavens,
We too, could be
Free ...

(LIGHTS rise on OLD NOLAN, CLARKIE, and LEON at the reception.)

ELDER LEON.
Until we are but tiny specks in the heavens,
We too, could be
Free ...
    ROSCOE. Hey Eagles! Who's the boss?
    OTHERS. The 99th.

ROSCOE. Who's the king?
OTHERS. The 99th.
ROSCOE. Who can't be beat?
OTHERS. The 99th.
ELDER NOLAN. They tried everything they could to discredit us.
ELDER CLARKIE. Even after they couldn't hold us any longer.
ELDER NOLAN. I thought as soon as we got home and stepped off the boat things would be different! But we did change some things, didn't we?
ELDER LEON. Indeed we did.
ELDER CLARK. Well Eagles, are we ready to go?

(ELDER NOLAN starts the drill.)

ELDER LEON. You're not going to do what I think you're gonna do, are you?
ELDER NOLAN. That's right. The Jitterbug Drill? (*HE begins to dance.*) You see me? You see me, don't you? Come on, you all, don't leave me out here all by myself now.
ELDER LEON. Shoot, you made your bed, brother, now lie in it. You can fool yourself if you want to, but you're not going to fool me into a bottle of liniment tomorrow.
ELDER NOLAN. Come on, Clarkie. Look at me. Haven't lost one step.
ELDER LEON. That's right, you've lost several steps. Brother, you have lost a whole lot of steps.
ELDER NOLAN. Come on, Clarkie.
ELDER CLARKIE. All right, here I come. Here I

come. Look out now. Look out!

ELDER LEON. I'm looking but I don't see anything.

ELDER CLARKIE. At my age I have to rev up the engine before I can move the car. (*HE moves into the dance with Nolan.*)

ELDER NOLAN. All right, less talking and more executing.

(CLARKIE stops.)

ELDER LEON. All right, so I'll splash on some liniment in the morning. Look out, Eagles, make room for Leon, because Leon is on his way!

ELDER CLARKIE. The Jitterbug Drill!

ELDER NOLAN. These young folks today better learn it. They just might need it one day.

ELDER LEON. It'll help them through some hard times.

ELDER CLARKIE. When they learn the Drill, then we'll leave them on their own. Paving the way. Right, Eagles?

ELDER LEON. That's right!

ELDERS. Paving the way! Just paving the way.

(ELDERS marching in time as LIGHTS fade to black.)

THE END

FURNITURE AND PROPS

6 cots
6 footlockers
Finished sculpture
6 chairs
Bottle of cognac (full)
Barracks phonograph
Small notebook and pen
Square metal table for phonograph
2 lighters
Slide projector with gel slides
Matches
Low wicker stand for projector
Lucky Strikes
Large wooden crate
Pia's bed
Square sculpture table
Short stool
Wash basin with stand and towel
Wind-up Phonograph
Square wooden phonograph table
Julius
6 V-discs in sleeves
2 rags
7 conical paper cups
3 scotch glasses
**3 cans shoe polish
**2 shoe brushes
**Towel & rag
Baseball
**Assorted clippings

2 newspapers
4 *Time Magazines*
3 Postcards
4 small metal ashtrays
**Box of envelopes
Writing paper
Pen
Brown folder
Photo of Lisa
Map
**Navigational instruments
**Protractor/compass
Unfinished sculpture with cover
Block of clay
Assorted sculpting tools in jar
3 records in sleeves
Suitcase
Deck of cards
Photo of Lena Horne
3 empty uncapped beer bottles
4 half full uncapped beer bottles
3 full capped beer bottles in bucket
2 bottle openers
Folder with Momyers' report
General's envelope with Anzio orders
Clipboard with statement (pen attached.)
Tin canister with bottle of Coca-cola

** DENOTES PROPS IN FOOTLOCKERS NOT ACTUALLY USED

Act I Preset

All furniture to Act I spikes
Footlocker Props as per diagram
4 V-discs in sleeves under barracks phonograph
Rag under barracks phonograph
7 conical cups under barracks phonograph.
V-disc ready to fall on barracks phonograph
Elder Nolan's glass on SL chair (all glasses full)
Elder Clarkie's glass under projector
Elder Leon's glass under his chair
Projector <u>ON</u> with first slide in gate
Julius at foot of Roscoe's bed
Unfinished sculpture covered on table
Sculpting tools on table in jar
Pack of cigarettes (one out) on table
Matches and ashtray on table
Block of clay on table
Rag on lower shelf of table
Suitcase under Pia's bed
Bedclothes turned down
Phonograph cranked with brake on
3 records in sleeves under Phonograph

WARDROBE:
Elder Leon's jacket on his chair
Roscoe's baseball cap in his trunk
Othel's crush cap in his trunk
Pia's robe on SL bedpost
Buddy's shirt and jacket on SR bedpost

OFFSTAGE:
Deck of cards
Lena Horne
3 empty beer bottles
4 full beer bottles
General's folder
General's envelope
Clipboard with pen attached
Tin with Coca-cola
3 *Time Magazines*
Newspaper
3 postcards

PERSONAL PROPS:
Leon—notebook, pen, matches, cigarettes
Clarkie—bottle opener, lighter, cigarettes
Whitson—lighter, cigarettes
Buddy—matches, cigarettes

Intermission Preset

STRIKE:
1 chair
Othel's footlocker
Suitcase
Unfinished sculpture
Cigarettes, matches, ashtray from Pia's
Extension cord

SET:
All furniture to Act II spikes
Cognac bottle in Roscoe's trunk

V-disc in sleeve at foot of Othel's bed
Bucket with 3 capped bottles (opener attached) on Buddy's trunk
Record "playing" on barracks phonograph
Ashtray on Buddy's bed
Ashtray on Leon's trunk
Ashtray on Clarkie's trunk
Finished sculpture on table
Sculpting tools on table with rag
Sculpture cover on shelf under table
Record playing on Pia's Phonograph with needle on
Phonograph cranked with brake on
Bed made
Block of clay on table

OFFSTAGE:
Refilled scotch glasses for Elders

WARDROBE:
Flight suits, helmets, scarves, gloves, harnesses in trunks
Buddy's jacket at the foot of Othel's bed

BLACK EAGLES

Footlockers - Hand props and
Wardrobe presets Act I

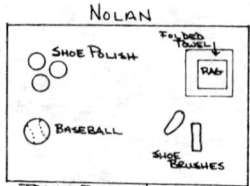

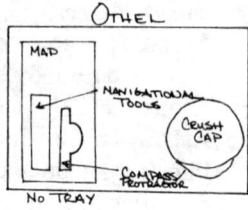

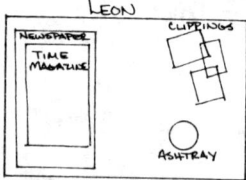

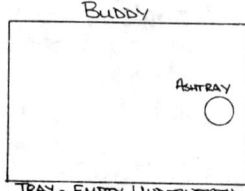

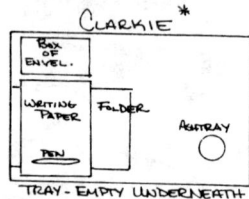

* LISA'S PHOTO IN SLEEVE
UNDER LID

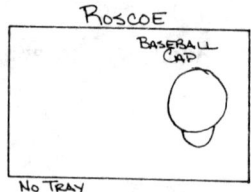

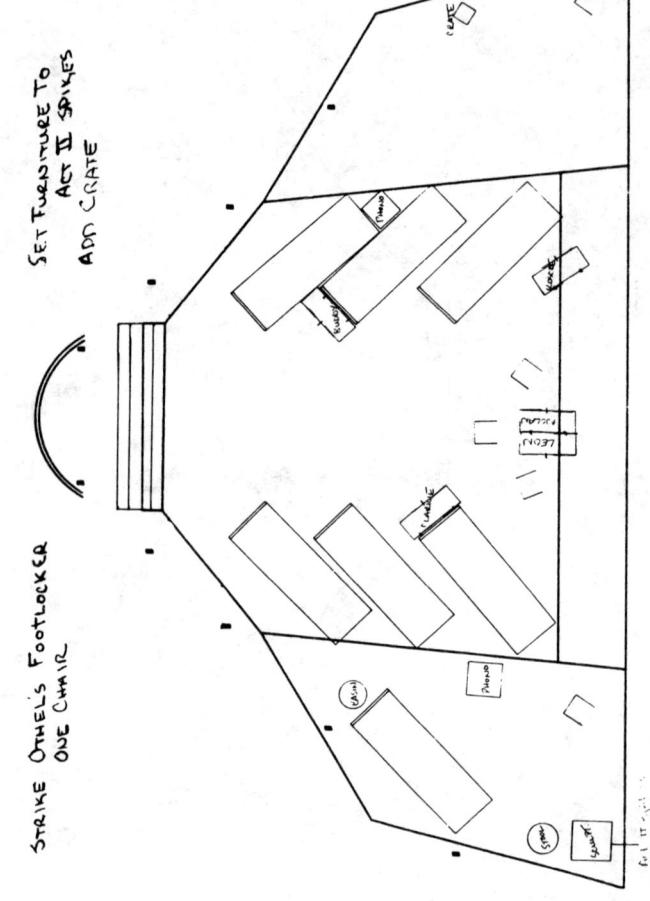

A RAISIN IN THE SUN
By LORRAINE HANSBERRY
DRAMA
7 men, 3 women, 1 child—Interior

A Negro family is cramped in a flat on the south side of Chicago. They are a widow, her son (a chauffeur), his wife, his sister, and his little boy. The widow is expecting a $10,000 insurance settlement on her husband's death, and her son is constantly begging her to give him the money so that he can become co-owner of a liquor store. He wants to quit chauffeuring, to become a business man, and to be able to leave his son a little bit more than his own father, a bricklayer, had left him: this is the only way a Negro can continue to improve his lot. The widow, meantime, has placed a down-payment on a house where they can have sunlight, and be rid of roaches. The despair of the young husband is intense. His mother reluctantly turns over the remaining $6500 to him, as head of the house. He invests in the liquor store, his partner absconds, and his dream is forever dead. A representative from the better (white) neighborhood, into which they planned to move, calls on them and offers to reimburse them handsomely for their investment. But our young man now realizes that a little bit of dignity is all he can ever count on, and he plans to move his family to the new house.

PURLIE VICTORIOUS
By OSSIE DAVIS
COMEDY
6 men, 3 women—Exterior, 2 comp.

By taking all the cliches of plays, about the lovable old south and the love that existed between white masters and colored slaves, Ossie Davis has compounded a constantly comic play. Purlie Victorious has come back to his shabby cabin to announce that he will reacquire the local church and ring the freedom bell. There is an inheritance due to a colored cousin, which would be sufficient to buy the church, but unfortunately it also is controlled by the white-head plantation colonel. Purlie Victorious tries to send a newcomer to the colonel to impersonate the heiress, not only is she found out, but the colonel makes a pass at her. Eventually the church is recovered, services are again held in it, and the freedom bell rings. It is the dialogue, though, that makes the events so uproarious ("Are you trying to get non-violent with me, boy?") or human ("Oh, child, being colored can be a lot of fun when they ain't nobody looking"). There's uncommonly good sense in such a line as the one delivered to Purlie when he was about to beat the colonel with the colonel's well-worn bullwhip: "You can't do wrong just because it's right."

Other Publications for Your Interest

SPELL #7
(BLACK THEATRE GROUPS—CHOREOPOEM)
By NTOZAKE SHANGE, music by BUTCH MORRIS and DAVID MURRAY

4 men, 5 women—Interior

Another striking "choreopoem" from the pen of the author of *For Colored Girls...!* This one is set in St. Louis, in a bar frequented by Black artists and musicians, and is yet another meditation on the irony of being Black in a White world. Shange has her artists bare their souls in soliloquies, many of them illustrated by in-the-mood dances. "Spell #7 is humanely upbeat. In the end, (it) proclaims inner self-respect as the essential quality of black pride and black identity."—Christian Science Monitor. "An extremely fine theatre piece."—N.Y. Daily News. "A most lovely and powerful work."—N.Y. Times.

FOR COLORED GIRLS WHO HAVE CONSIDERED SUICIDE/WHEN THE RAINBOW IS ENUF
(LITTLE THEATRE)
By NTOZAKE SHANGE

7 women—Bare stage

For Colored Girls... is a passionately feminist spellbinder, a fluidly staged collection of vivid narrative pieces, some in prose and some in free verse, performed by seven young black women. It is almost exclusively concerned with the cavalier and sometimes downright brutal treatment accorded black women by their men. The play also captures the inner feelings of today's black women and goes beyond that to achieve its own kind of universality. Though their performances are mainly solo, the girls are united in much the same way as the cast in "A Chorus Line"—sometimes they sing together and on occasion dance together. And they are always united in sorrow, spirit, pride and soul. "...a triumphant event...filled with humor...joyous and alive, affirmative in the face of despair, and pure theatre."—N.Y. Daily News. "...a poignant, gripping, angry and beautiful theatre work."—Time. "...bitingly alive...overwhelming in its emotional impact...tragic, funny, proud and compassionate...."—Newsweek.

Other Publications for Your Interest

A LESSON FROM ALOES
(LITTLE THEATRE—DRAMA)
By ATHOL FUGARD

2 men, 1 woman—Interior

N.Y. Drama Critics Circle Award, Best Play of the Year. Set in a house in a white district of Port Elizabeth, South Africa, in 1963 this important new work by a truly major dramatist gives a compelling portrait of a society caught in the grip of a police state, and the effect it has on individuals. We are in the house of a liberal Afrikaner and his wife. He has been actively involved in anti-apartheid activity; she is recovering from a recent nervous breakdown brought about by a police raid on their home. They are waiting for a Black family to come to dinner (in South Africa, this is an absolutely forbidden act of insurrection). The Black family never arrives, but the head of the family does. He has just been released from prison and plans to flee South Africa—after first confronting the Afrikaner with the charge that he has betrayed him. "Exile, madness, utter loneliness—these are the only alternatives Mr. Fugard's characters have. What makes 'Aloes' so moving is the playwright's insistence on the heroism and integrity of these harsh choices."—N.Y. Times. "Immensely moving."—N.Y. Post. "One of the few dramatists in the world whose work really matters."—Newsweek. (#14146)

MEETINGS
(BLACK GROUPS—COMEDY)
By MUSTAPHA MATURA

1 man, 2 women—Interiors

Greatly-acclaimed in its recent Off-Broadway production at New York's excellent Phoenix Theatre, *Meetings* is set in an ultra-modern kitchen which would be the dream of any American family—but it is in fast-developing Trinidad and is well-stocked with everything but food, much to the consternation of the husband, a successful engineer. His wife, an equally successful marketing executive, spends too much time at "meetings" (so does he)—and neither has time to actually *use* their kitchen. While the husband pines for some good down-home cooking, the wife is off pushing a new brand of cigarette ("Trini" is being used as a test-market). Soon, the local people are coughing up blood, and many die—apparently from the effects of smoking the new cigarette. Eventually, the husband goes "back to nature" and the wife succumbs to her own product. "An amazing piece of theatre... a highly literal parable about the poisoning of the tropical isle by modern commercialism."—Women's Wear Daily. "A bright, sharp comedy that turns into a sombre fable before our eyes."—The New Yorker. (#15659)

Other Publications for Your Interest

LONG TIME SINCE YESTERDAY
(BLACK GROUPS—DRAMA)
By P.J. GIBSON

8 women—2 Interiors (may be unit set)

Set in suburban Camden, NJ in the early 1980's, this potent new drama by a talented new Black playwright is about a reunion of former college mates, now in their thirties, at the funeral of another friend, who has recently killed herself. These women are prosperous, professional, middle-class Black women who have gone through the turbulence of the sixties and have come out on top in the eighties. These are women you know. At the wake for their sadly deceased friend, the women finally confront the truth about their own lives, and about the suicide which has once again brought them together. All eight roles in the play are well-defined and, needless to say, are quite juicy parts for actresses. This is a literate, humorous, sensitive look at the lives of eight contemporary Black women. It was a SRO success at New York City's New Federal Theatre, which has started so many Black plays and playwrights on the road to recognition. We heartily, fervently recommend *Long Time Since Yesterday*. (#14646)

HUNTER
(BLACK GROUPS—DRAMA)
By NUBA-HAROLD STUART

2 men, 2 women (all blacks)—Interior

This moving and, at times, very humorous new drama is about Jerri, a Black mother, and her new boyfriend, Jake. He has spent the night with Jerri at her house. Jerri fixes him a good down-home breakfast—and introduces him to her teen-aged son, Hunter. Naturally, Jake's pretty surprised to hear that Jerri *has* a son. He is even *more* surprised—and filled with consternation—when Hunter comes to breakfast—for Hunter is severely brain-damaged. Jake then has to make a big decision—just how much does he care for Jerri? This touching new play, a *must* for all college, Black and community theatre groups, was a recent success at New York City's famed Actors Studio. The universality of its subject matter makes *Hunter* a sure winner. (#10162)